VEGAN ITALIAN FOOD

BY SHANNON MARTINEZ.

Hardie Grant

BOOKS

INTRODUCTION

It might seem strange that I am writing an Italian cookbook when my last name is Martinez, but I promise you that I am not doing this to capitalise on trends or to appropriate someone else's culture. When I grew up in Melbourne in the eighties, Welcomed Overseas Guests – or WOGs, as we affectionately call ourselves – were all seen as the same. Spanish, Italian, Greek, Maltese, Egyptian – we were all wogs. We all lived in the same areas, bought our groceries from the same specialty stores, hung out and cooked together. It was a safety-in-numbers thing, and a hanging-out-where-good-food-could-be-found thing.

To be clear: I love Italian food. I love the seasonal philosophy of its cooking. I love taking an absolute glut of produce at its peak and eating it raw, cooking it down to a pulp, preserving and jarring it. I love the inherently frugal nature of the cuisine, where dishes are formed out of necessity and by intuition as much as by tradition. It is what makes Italian food so impossibly tasty and accessible as well as affordable to cook. As a proud first-generation Spanish-Australian, I love buying fruit and vegetables that have to be processed *today*, or they'll be spoiled tomorrow, at a fraction of the cost (or even free) and locking in all the flavour and nutrients at the optimum point of eating. One of my fondest memories growing up was haggling for boxes of produce at Preston Market in Melbourne near closing time, and it is a tradition that I still carry on to this day. I love it so much that I even have a tattoo dedicated to this philosophy: NPFP.

Never
Pay
Full
Price

It's a philosophy that is rooted in all cuisines with peasant food: you cook with what is abundantly available, in the most delicious way possible and bulk it out with carbs. Another benefit of this style of cooking is that it is already vegan. It is vegan by necessity. It's accidentally vegan. If you asked any of the nonnas I grew up with if they knew they were cooking vegan food, they'd respond by asking, 'What is vegan?'

It's no secret that I am not vegan, but I still eat a plant-based diet 95 per cent of the time. *This* is the type of vegan food that I love to eat: dried beans, pulses and legumes cooked to a pulp, infused with aromatics and wiped up with soft, crusty bread. I love my bitter leaves braised to within an inch of their lives in healthy glugs of olive oil until the pepperiness of the oil and the vegetal characteristics of the greens become one.

My goal for this book is to focus on the breadth of dishes that already exist in Italian cuisine that don't require veganising. This is vegan food in its purest form.

That being said, I know fans of my venues Smith & Daughters and Smith & Deli would revolt if I didn't include my recipes for salami, cacio e pepe and tiramisu. Never fear, they're in here. And before I hear an Italian say I've made their ancestors roll over in their graves from my recipes, the nature of veganising these dishes will always inevitably be inauthentic. What I *can* guarantee is, if you feed them to your nonna, she won't be able to tell the difference.

Shannon

A NOTE ON MY RECIPES

Oil: I am generous with it. I don't see it as unhealthy when eaten in moderation and it really does give dishes body and carry flavour. If my quantities are too much for you, feel free to reduce it to your personal preference. But just between us, my grandmother consumed so much olive oil she practically bathed in it and had the skin of a cherub until her dying day. Do with that information what you will.

As with most recipes, if you don't like an herb or a supporting ingredient, don't use it. Substitute it for something you *do* like. Just know that once you make a change, it is now your recipe and not mine and will not taste the way it was intended.

When I specify 'small' jars, I'm referring to 250 ml (8½ fl oz/1 cup). Large jars are 500 ml (17 fl oz/2 cups). If you feel that many of the recipes, especially in the Condimenti chapter, make a LOT, it's because I want you to be able to make them once a year and have them last. If you want, you can halve the recipes to suit your preference.

If you're accustomed to canning and feel confident in your preserving practice, almost all jarred recipes in this book can be stored in the pantry. To sterilise your jars (and their lids), wash them thoroughly in soapy water and place in the oven at 120°C (250°F) open side-down until completely dry. This will probably take about 10 minutes. But if you can't be bothered – or want to be on the safe side – store in the fridge instead. I don't want my recipes to be the reason for your hospital visit.

I've used grams for liquid measurements in many of the baking, fresh dough, gelato and granita recipes for accuracy. Trust me, being exact with the ingredients in these recipes is worth it – just get yourself some good digital scales.

Lastly, my portions are not for small eaters. I write recipes as if I am feeding my own family. These are Martinez portions. If you're not a big eater, halve the recipes or make space in your freezer. All mains can be frozen for future.

Note

This book uses 20 ml (¾ fl oz) tablespoons. Cooks using 15 ml (½ fl oz) tablespoons should be mindful of slightly increasing the amount with their tablespoon measurements. Metric cup measurements are used, i.e. 250 ml for 1 cup; in the US a cup is 8 fl oz, just smaller, so American cooks should be generous in their cup measurements.

Additionally, the recipes in this book were cooked in a fan-forced or convection oven, so if using a conventional oven, increase the temperature by 20°C (35°F).

The basics: you gotta master 'em. As they say, you have to know how to walk before you can run, and this chapter is the walking. The chapters that follow are the running.

The basics I am talking about here are beans, legumes and dried mushrooms. These key elements are the backbone of all good vegan cooking. Being able to manipulate them is a skill that will stay with you for a lifetime.

Sadly, not all of you got the opportunity to cook with your grandma on Sundays, so these lessons were never passed down to you.

That's where I come in.

Think of my guide as the sassy nonna you never had, and you'll never eat a busted bean or tasteless shroom again.

COOKING 101

DRIED LEGUMES & PULSES

Okay. Stay with me. I know that I may seem like I'm preaching to the choir, seeing as this is a vegan book and all, but after speaking to a lot of people, I was amazed by how many didn't know the correct way to cook dried pulses and legumes. Like all things, there's a right way and a wrong way to do it. So, this section will ensure you know the right way. Freshly cooked beans are far superior to tinned, both in flavour and texture. They're also a hell of a lot cheaper than the tinned varieties. Don't get me wrong, I have a pantry full of tinned beans of every variety and use them frequently when I'm strapped for time and need to eat. On the other hand, tinned lentils will never enter my house. If I have the time to plan my meals ahead, it's dried all the way for me. Here's an in-depth guide on how to cook them.

What we're cooking

Dried pulses or legumes (e.g. lentils, chickpeas, borlotti (cranberry) beans, cannellini beans, kidney beans), aromatic vegetables and spices (optional, for flavour)

What you'll need

Large pot with a lid
Colander or strainer
Water

HOW TO DO IT

Sort and rinse

First things first: grab your dried legumes and give them a good look over. Pick out any rocks, twigs or suspicious-looking characters, then rinse them like you're washing away their secrets.

Soaking (optional)

Some legumes benefit from soaking, which can reduce cooking time and make them more digestible. Soaking is particularly useful for beans like chickpeas, kidney beans and black beans. You have two methods to choose from here:

Overnight soak: Place the rinsed legumes in a large bowl and cover with plenty of cold water. Soak overnight, or for 8–12 hours. Drain and rinse before cooking.

Quick soak: Place the rinsed legumes in a pot, cover with water and bring to the boil. Boil for 2–3 minutes, then remove from the heat, cover and let them soak for 1–2 hours. Drain and rinse.

Cooking

Place the soaked or unsoaked legumes in a large pot and add enough water to cover them by at least 10 cm (4 in). If you like, you can add some aromatic vegetables like onions, garlic or bay leaves for extra flavour. Do not add salt at this stage, as it can toughen the legumes.

Place the pot on the stove over a high heat and bring the water to a rapid boil. Once boiling, reduce the heat to low and let the legumes simmer. Cover the pot with a lid but leave it slightly ajar to allow steam to escape. Check the water level occasionally, adding more if needed to keep the legumes well submerged.

Cooking times

Cooking times will vary depending on the type of legume you're cooking, but use this as a guide:

Lentils: 20–30 minutes
Chickpeas: 1.5–2 hours
Beans: 1–1.5 hours

Test for doneness by looking at the texture. They should be tender but not mushy. Season them with salt. Any beans that you wish to store in the fridge or freezer should be stored in their cooking liquid.

Remember that exact cooking times will vary, so it's important to taste and test the legumes as you go. The age of the legumes will also have an impact on the end result. Old beans are not going to cook well. If you've cooked a pot of beans in the past and they have turned to mush, there's a good chance they were old and stale. So, if you don't plan on cooking them often, buy them in small quantities and restock when you need them.

Season and serve

Remove any aromatics you may have added earlier, and serve.

Enjoy

Your cooked legumes are now ready to be used in a whole bunch of dishes such as soups, stews, salads, or as a side dish. Store any leftover beans in an airtight container covered in their cooking liquid in the fridge for up to 3 days or freeze for up to 6 months.

DRIED MUSHROOMS

Drying mushrooms is the best way to preserve their flavour and extend their shelf life. Whether you forage for wild mushrooms or have a surplus from the markets, here's a guide on how to dry them.

What we're cooking

Fresh mushrooms (wild or cultivated)

What you'll need

A sharp knife
A clean, soft brush or paper towel
Dehydrator or oven
Airtight containers or vacuum-sealed bags

HOW TO DO IT

Selecting mushrooms

You can dry most varieties. Just be sure to choose fresh, firm mushrooms that are free from any decay or mould. No drying those musty old mushrooms in the bottom of your veg' drawer in the fridge.

Cleaning the mushrooms

Gently brush off any dirt or debris using a soft brush, or wipe the mushrooms clean with a slightly damp paper towel. Avoid soaking them in water, as mushrooms are like sponges and will absorb moisture, which can affect the drying process.

Slicing or preparing

Depending on the size and type of mushrooms, you can slice them uniformly to ensure even drying. Thinly sliced mushrooms dry faster and more evenly.

Dehydrator method

Using a dehydrator is the most convenient option for drying mushrooms. Arrange the mushroom slices in a single layer on the dehydrator trays. Set the temperature to around 55°C (131°F) and let them dry for 6–12 hours, depending on the thickness of the slices and the moisture content of the mushrooms. Check the mushrooms every few hours and remove them when they become crisp and brittle.

Oven method

If you don't have a dehydrator, you can use your oven or, even better, a wood-fired oven. The benefit of a wood-fired oven is that your dried mushrooms will get a beautiful smoky flavour. Preheat the oven to its lowest setting. This is usually around 65°C (149°F). Place the mushroom slices on baking trays in a single layer. Prop the oven door open slightly with a wooden spoon to allow moisture to escape. Bake for 3–6 hours, checking them regularly, until they are thoroughly dried and crispy.

Cooling and storing

Let the dried mushrooms cool to room temperature before handling. Store them in airtight containers or vacuum-sealed bags to keep them fresh and free from moisture.

Rehydrating mushrooms

To use your dried mushrooms in recipes, rehydrate them by soaking them in warm water for about 20–30 minutes. Save the soaking liquid, as it can be used to add flavour to soups, braises, risottos and sauces.

When you are a vegan chef, sometimes you have no alternative but to make your products from scratch. What's available on the shelf is either too dry, too rubbery, too processed, too bland, or not fit for human consumption. Or it just plain doesn't exist.

In this chapter, I also teach you how to process a glut of produce, because I think the art of preservation is slowly dying out due to industrialisation. Every time I jar up tomatoes or dry produce in the sun, I imagine myself preparing for the zombie apocalypse.

These recipes might be quite involved, but they will have infinite applications throughout this book and in your own cooking (they're also the bases of my most popular dishes). Think of these techniques as life skills that will make your existence infinitely more delicious.

BUILDING BLOCKS

PASSATA

Few ingredients, many methods. Life skillz – 100! Don't let anyone tell you you're a hoarder by stashing jars away all year. They won't complain when you rock up to their house with a box full of passata.

**MAKES APPROX.
5 LITRES (169 FL OZ)**

5 kg (11 lb) very ripe tomatoes
250 ml (8½ fl oz/1 cup) water
2 tablespoons salt flakes
½ bunch of basil

Sterilise five 1 litre (34 fl oz/4 cups) jars.

Wash the tomatoes well. Using a sharp pointed knife, remove the cores from the tomatoes, then cut in half.

Squeeze the tomatoes over a bowl to remove the seeds and excess liquid.

Add the water to a very large stockpot, followed by the tomatoes. If you don't have a large enough pot, split the water and tomatoes over two smaller ones.

Cover the pot with a lid and cook the tomatoes over a very low heat, stirring every 5–10 minutes until they become very pulpy. This will take anywhere between 20–30 minutes.

Pour the tomato pulp into a large colander in the sink and allow as much excess water to drain out as possible.

Set a large bowl under a moulie, passata machine or passata attachment for a stand mixer and ladle in the cooked tomatoes in batches. Once you have passed all the tomatoes through the mill, collect the skins and any pulp that has not gone into the bowl, and pass it again to make sure you've gotten every last drop of tomato goodness out. Stir in the salt.

Line up your sterilised bottles or jars and place a small sprig of basil in each one.

Using a funnel, fill each bottle with the passata, leaving about 2 cm (¾ in) of space at the top. Seal tightly with the lid.

Clean out the stockpot and carefully place the bottles in. Cover with water and bring to the boil. Boil for 20 minutes, then turn off the heat and allow the water to cool to room temperature before removing the bottles. If sealed correctly, you can store the bottles in the pantry pretty much indefinitely. Once opened, use within 4 days.

If you don't want to jar your passata, you can freeze it in containers or resealable bags.

tomatoes (as few or as many as you
like and that will fit in your smoker)

extra-virgin olive oil, for drizzling

1 garlic clove per 1 kg (2 lb 3 oz)
tomatoes

2 thyme sprigs per 1 kg (2 lb 3 oz)
tomatoes

¼ teaspoon dried oregano per 1 kg
(2 lb 3 oz) tomatoes

SMOKED TOMATOES

I understand this recipe isn't going to be for everyone, but I
wanted to include it because it's bloody delicious. This is one
of those recipes that you want to make when tomatoes are in
season and at their peak. If you're fortunate to have a backyard
pizza oven or smoker, this one's for you. Get smokin'.

Heat the smoker to 100°C (210°F).

Cut the tomatoes in half, through the core. If they are very large, cut
into quarters.

Place the tomato in a large bowl and drizzle lightly with olive oil. Add the
remaining ingredients and toss well to coat.

Place on a perforated tray or rack, cut side up, and put into the smoker.
Smoke for 1–2 hours depending on how strong you like the smoky flavour.

Remove from the smoker and use as is. This will result in a smoky yet still
juicy tomato. Or you can dry them following the recipe on page 36 to
preserve and intensify the flavour.

'NDUJA

50 g (1¾ oz) dry dark textured
    vegetable protein

150 ml (5 fl oz) hot vegan beef stock

150 g (5½ oz) vegetable shortening

½ small brown onion, finely diced

5 garlic cloves, finely minced

1–2 tablespoons fermented chilli paste,
    or 1–2 red chillies

1 teaspoon ground fennel

1–2 teaspoons chilli flakes

1 tablespoon smoked paprika

1 tablespoon sweet paprika

100 g (3½ oz) Sun-dried tomatoes
    (page 36)

50 g (1¾ oz) dried shiitake mushrooms,
    rehydrated for 1 hour in hot water

100 ml (3½ fl oz) mushroom soaking
    liquid

50 ml (1¾ fl oz) red-wine vinegar

100 g (3½ oz) cooked kidney beans,
    fresh or tinned

1 tablespoon red miso paste

2 teaspoons salt flakes

extra-virgin olive oil

Once you make this, you can use it across a bunch of different recipes: as a spread in a sandwich, dot it on pizza or cook it down in the base of a pasta sauce. Think of this spreadable salami as a fiery umami bomb for anything you add it to.

In a small bowl, soak the textured vegetable protein in the hot beef stock.

While that's soaking, melt the vegetable shortening in a large frying pan over a medium heat, then add the onion. Add a big pinch of salt and fry for 5 minutes, or until soft and lightly golden.

Add the garlic and cook for another minute, then add the fermented chilli paste, ground fennel, chilli flakes, smoked paprika and sweet paprika. Season and stir well to combine, then cook for another minute.

Transfer the mixture to a food processor and add all the remaining ingredients, except the olive oil. Blend until smooth, then return to the frying pan.

Cook over a low heat for 5–10 minutes, stirring continuously until the mixture has dried out and it resembles a thick paste. Adjust the seasoning to taste then place in a container. Top with enough olive oil to cover the surface of the 'nduja, then refrigerate.

Allow the flavours to develop for a minimum of 24 hours before using. It will keep for 2 weeks in the fridge in an airtight container.

RICOTTA

1 litre (34 fl oz/4 cups) soy milk

1 teaspoon salt flakes

a few cracks of white pepper

60 ml (2 fl oz/¼ cup) white-wine vinegar

extra-virgin olive oil, for drizzling (optional)

sea salt flakes, to taste (optional)

We've come a long way in the vegan cheese world in the last five years, but the good cheeses are still few and far between – and I say that living in a major city. So, I wanted to give you a fail-safe ricotta recipe that you can access 24/7 using ingredients you can even find at a gas station.

Heat the soy milk in a saucepan over a medium heat until bubbles begin to form around the side of the pan – don't let it simmer or boil. Turn off the heat, add the salt and pepper and slowly pour in the vinegar.

Gently pass a spatula or spoon through the milk only a few times. Leave to sit for 1 hour.

Line a sieve with a piece of muslin (cheesecloth), or any thin cloth, and set the sieve over a bowl. Pour the milk into the sieve, then refrigerate and leave to drain for at least 12 hours, preferably overnight.

Remove the ricotta from the cloth and store in an airtight container in the fridge for up to 5 days.

MASCARPONE

1 litre (34 fl oz/4 cups) soy milk
  (as natural as possible)
pinch of salt
60 ml (2 fl oz/¼ cup) lemon juice
150 ml (5 fl oz) vegan cream
1 tablespoon icing (confectioners')
  sugar

This recipe is great in both sweet and savoury applications, and you absolutely must master it if you want to replicate the ultra-luxe Smith & Daughters version of the Tiramisu (page 205) at home.

Heat the soy milk in a saucepan over a medium heat just until bubbles begin to form around the side of the pan – don't let it simmer or boil. Turn off the heat, add the salt, then slowly pour in the lemon juice.

Gently pass a spatula or spoon through the milk only a few times. Leave to sit for 1 hour.

Using a slotted spoon, carefully lift out the curds and place in a sieve lined with muslin (cheesecloth) – or any other thin cloth – and set over a bowl. Fold the edges of the cloth over the top of the mixture and refrigerate for at least 12 hours, or overnight.

Once the curds have drained and solidified, drop them into a food processor and add the cream and icing sugar. Blend until smooth, then pour into a container and seal with the lid. Refrigerate for at least another 4 hours before using.

In Italy, aperitivo is the ritual of consuming drinks and snacks designed to 'open up' your stomach for dinner. It's one of my favourite activities, but we don't have much of a culture of it in Australia.

When I think of aperitivo, it's the bunch of snacks I have at home before a night out. It's the collection of different plates I can pick from when I am getting dressed, doing my makeup and sipping on a drink. I may or may not have dinner plans, so I have to line my stomach for the shenanigans ahead. Think of it as pre-drinks but for food: a guaranteed good time and sometimes better than the main event.

The best aperitivo contains a selection of hot, cold and ambient-temperature snacks, so pick and choose a few recipes from this chapter to serve at a time. I like to enjoy mine with Casa Mariol Vermut Negro on the rocks with an orange twist, but there are no rules to aperitivo – choose your own adventure.

APERITIVO

TOMATO GRANITA

2.5 kg (5½ lb) ripe tomatoes
(a mixture of varieties for
extra flavour, if possible),
roughly chopped

10 g (¼ oz) salt flakes

10–15 ml (¼–½ fl oz) sherry vinegar

20–30 g (¾–1 oz) sugar
(depending on the sweetness
of your tomatoes)

½ red chilli, deseeded and roughly
chopped (optional)

a few cracks of white pepper

I love to serve this as a refreshing palate cleanser on hot days, drizzled with a little extra-virgin olive oil and a sprinkling of salt flakes. This is also delicious on top of a chilled soup or Bloody Mary.

In a large bowl, toss the chopped tomatoes with the salt flakes and crush with your hands for about 1 minute, or until you have a chunky, soupy texture. Add the sherry vinegar, sugar, chilli and white pepper and massage again to ensure it's well combined.

Cover and allow to sit at room temperature for a minimum of 3 hours, or preferably overnight. Give the mixture a little massage every now and then to help the liquids release.

When you're ready to make the granita, place a shallow-sided metal tray in the freezer to chill.

Next, working in batches, add the tomato mixture to a blender and blitz until you have a chunky soup texture – no need to blend till super smooth.

Line a fine-mesh sieve with muslin (cheesecloth), or any clean fine-mesh cloth, and place the sieve over a bowl.

Sieve the tomato puree in batches. Squeeze down on the tomato pulp then bring the corners of the cloth together and form a tomatoey sack. SQUEEZE. You're after every last drop of that delicious tomato water. Once all the liquid has been removed, set the pulp aside to use in passata, or mix with oil and garlic for a quick bruschetta topping.

Pour the tomato water into the tray and cover with plastic wrap. Freeze until the liquid begins to turn solid at the edges but is still slightly slushy in the middle.

Use a fork to break up the ice into smaller crystals, then return the tray to the freezer. Repeat this process every half hour until it's completely frozen and has the texture of snow. This should take between 2–4 hours.

PICKLED RADICCHIO

2 large heads radicchio, quartered
   with stalks intact

200 ml (7 fl oz) vegetable oil

200 ml (7 fl oz) extra-virgin olive oil

1 teaspoon chilli seeds

1 teaspoon fennel seeds

2 handfuls of fresh marjoram or
   oregano, leaves and stalks

½ brown onion, thinly sliced

1 tablespoon salt flakes

1 teaspoon ground black pepper

1 bay leaf

2 tablespoons soy sauce

500 ml (17 fl oz/2 cups) red-wine
   vinegar

zest of 1 orange

This recipe is my gateway drug to radicchio. A lot of people don't like bitter vegetables, but grilling and pickling them definitely softens the blow.

Heat a heavy chargrill pan or barbecue chargrill until very hot. If you don't have either of those, a heavy frying pan will do.

Place the radicchio pieces on the grill, cut side down. Cook until well charred on all sides, then place the wedges into a large bowl.

To make the pickle brine, combine all the remaining ingredients, except the soy sauce, vinegar and orange zest, in a large saucepan and bring to a simmer over a medium heat.

Take off the heat and leave to infuse. Once it reaches room temperature, add the remaining ingredients and stir to combine.

Remove and discard the cores from the radicchio and place the leaves in a large jar, container or vacuum-pack bag. Pour the pickle liquid in, then seal.

Leave for at least 24 hours for the flavours to develop before eating. It can be eaten cold or warm.

Store in the fridge for up to 2 weeks.

MARINATED OLIVES

120 ml (4 fl oz) extra-virgin olive oil

¼ bunch of parsley, finely chopped

2 tablespoons red-wine vinegar

1 teaspoon dried oregano

1 rosemary sprig

5 whole black peppercorns

1 teaspoon fennel seeds

500 g (1 lb 2 oz) olives of your choice
   (a mixture of at least two varieties
   is always nice)

5 garlic cloves, peeled and smashed

2–3 whole dried chillies, slightly
   crushed, or ½ teaspoon chilli flakes

1 small lemon or orange, rind peeled
   into strips with a vegetable peeler

This is an easy way to make cheap olives exceptional.

In a mixing bowl whisk together all the ingredients, except the olives, garlic, chillies and citrus rind. Once well combined, add the remaining ingredients and stir well to coat.

Pour the olives and marinade into one large or several small jars and seal tightly. Marinate at room temperature for 24 hours before placing in the fridge to store. Once opened, the olives will keep for up to 1 month.

Note

Depending on the oil you use, it may solidify slightly once cold. If this happens, just pull the olives out of the fridge about 30 minutes before you want to eat them.

MARINATED CHARRED ARTICHOKES

Learning how to prepare artichokes is a great life skill. But if preparing artichokes isn't on your bucket list, feel free to use jarred artichokes and marinate them.

APERITIVO

MAKES APPROX.
750 G (1 LB 11 OZ)

1 large lemon, halved

5 large globe artichokes

3 bay leaves

5 garlic cloves, 4 smashed, 1 finely sliced, peeled first

5 whole black peppercorns

1 teaspoon salt

¼ bunch of parsley, roughly chopped, stalks reserved

3 thyme sprigs

½ teaspoon chilli flakes (optional)

80 ml (2½ fl oz/⅓ cup) chardonnay or white-wine vinegar

220 ml (7½ fl oz) extra-virgin olive oil

Fill a large saucepan or stockpot with about 2 litres (68 fl oz/8 cups) water. Squeeze the juice from the lemon halves directly into the water, then drop in the halves.

Remove the hard outer leaves from the artichokes, including the stalks. Keep picking the leaves until you get to the paler greenish-yellow leaves that are noticeably softer.

Trim the ends of the stalks leaving about 5 cm (2 in) of stalk from the base of the artichoke. Using either a knife or a vegetable peeler, peel the stalks until the tough outer layers have been removed.

Using a serrated knife, cut 2–3 cm (¾–1¼ in) off the top of each artichoke, then place in the pot of water as you go to avoid them browning.

Once all the artichokes are trimmed and in the pot, add the bay leaves, smashed garlic, peppercorns, salt and parsley stalks. Top up with water if necessary to cover the artichokes. Place an upturned plate on top of the artichokes to keep them submerged.

Bring to the boil over a high heat, then reduce the heat to low and simmer gently for about 45 minutes, or until the artichokes are tender and easily pierced by a sharp knife. Once cooked, drop the artichokes into a bowl of iced water and leave until they are cool enough to handle, then drain.

Stand the artichoke, stalk side up, on a chopping board and cut in half through the stem and head. Use a teaspoon to carefully remove the hairy choke inside the base of the head. Don't eat this!

At this point you could drop the artichokes straight into the marinade, but grilling them first gives a delicious smoky flavour and great texture. The choice is yours.

To grill, heat a chargrill pan or barbecue chargrill till very hot. Toss your blanched artichokes in a little olive oil, then grill until nicely charred.

Combine the remaining ingredients in a bowl. Place your cooked artichokes in whatever sealable container you like and pour the marinade over the top. Season to taste with salt and pepper, then seal the container and refrigerate for at least 12 hours before eating.

Store in the fridge for up to 2 weeks.

SALAMI

This is one of the original Smith & Deli recipes. It will give you a reliably good result without me physically coming to your home and showing you how to do it. If this if something you're after, please contact my agent. My rates are $5k an hour.

chilli flakes, for coating (optional)

Light marbling liquid

125 ml (4 fl oz/½ cup) water

½ tablespoon olive oil

½ tablespoon white miso paste

10 g (¼ oz) salt

20 g (¾ oz) caster (superfine) sugar

½ teaspoon vegan chicken stock powder

Dry ingredients for light dough

100 g (3½ oz) vital wheat gluten

20 g (¾ oz) onion powder

10 g (¼ oz) garlic powder

Dark marbling liquid

250 ml (8½ fl oz/1 cup) vegan beef stock

50 ml (1¾ fl oz) soy sauce

60 ml (2 fl oz/¼ cup) olive oil

60 g (2 oz) hot red pepper paste, or ajvar (Serbian roasted red pepper sauce)

30 g (1 oz) dark miso paste

25 ml (¾ fl oz) red-wine vinegar

15–30 ml (½–1 fl oz) hot sauce, to taste

25 g (1 oz) caster (superfine) sugar

25 g (1 oz) smoked paprika

2 garlic cloves, minced

Dry ingredients for dark dough

300 g (10½ oz) vital wheat gluten

20 g (¾ oz) onion powder

15 g (½ oz) smoked paprika

5 g (⅛ oz) freshly cracked black pepper

10 g (¼ oz) fennel seeds, crushed

¼ teaspoon dried oregano

10 g (¼ oz) beetroot powder (you can find this at most health food stores or online)

Start by blending the ingredients for the light marbling liquid in a blender until smooth. Transfer to a bowl.

Place all the dry ingredients for the light dough into another bowl and stir to combine, then pour into the blended mixture. Stir well, then knead for 5 minutes. Place the dough back in the bowl, cover and leave to rest for 1 hour.

Pour the ingredients for the dark marbling liquid into the blender (no need to rinse out) and blend until smooth.

Add the dry ingredients for the dark marbling dough to another large bowl and mix to combine, then pour in the wet mixture. Mix well, then knead for 5 minutes. Place the dough back in the bowl, cover and leave to rest for 1 hour.

After the doughs have rested, place the light dough on a chopping board and roughly dice it into small pieces about 2 cm (¾ in) square.

Add the pieces to the dark dough and lightly knead to combine. This will create a marbled effect.

Lay down one large sheet of baking paper on your benchtop. If you want the salami to be coated in chilli, sprinkle the paper with the chilli flakes. Cracked black pepper is also great.

Roughly form the dough into a large salami-shaped log, then place on the paper and roll it up. Twist the ends to seal.

Next, cut two large pieces of foil. Lay down the first one and wrap the rolled dough up in it tightly, then repeat with the second piece, twisting the ends to seal well.

To cook, set up a steamer basket large enough to hold the salami and set it above a pot of boiling water. Reduce to medium heat, cover and steam for one and a half hours. Occasionally check the water to make sure the pot isn't drying out.

Remove the salami from the steamer and allow to cool completely in the fridge overnight before slicing. This is important – don't skip this step!

This will store for longer if you keep it whole, up to a week. Best to slice it just before eating.

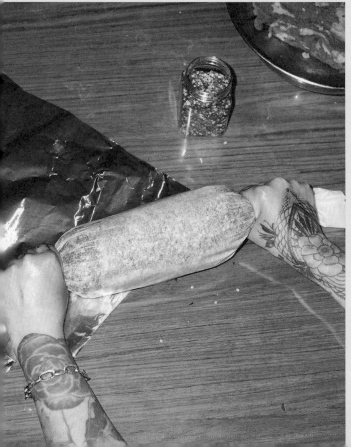

SUN-DRIED TOMATOES

You only need two ingredients: tomatoes and salt flakes.

This recipe is more a method, because once you've mastered the skills, you can just scale up or down. Have fun, enjoy and you'll be eating tomatoes all throughout the year.

Use whatever quantity of tomatoes you like. My only suggestion here is to do at least 3 kg (6 lb 10 oz). If you decide to actually use the sun-drying method, it takes time – not work, but time – so you may as well make a bunch and stock the pantry while the tomatoes are at their peak.

The preparation of the tomatoes is the same for both methods. Cut the tomatoes in half through where the stem would be. (Remove that little tomato belly button as well if you feel the need. It's nice but not necessary.) Lightly sprinkle the cut sides with salt flakes. THAT'S IT!

Once you have your very own sun-dried tomatoes, you can cover them with oil and your favourite herbs, maybe some garlic and a little chilli. Fully dry them and they can be jarred or stored in vacuum-sealed bags and kept in your pantry for ages. Hot tip: grinding fully dried tomatoes into a powder makes for a delicious addition to most things. Think of it as homemade MSG.

Sun-drying method

If you're not in a rush and have access to a yard or even a balcony, I strongly suggest you use this method. Just looking at them drying outside the window makes ya' feel like you've made nonnas around the world proud.

There are so many ways to MacGyver a sun-drying situation. I recently saw someone use an enclosed hanging tiered basket, which is definitely on my to-buy list once summer hits.

But the basic principle is that you need to create a system where air can circulate around the whole surface of the tomato. A baking tray with a rack on top works perfectly. But seriously, if you're going to do this, go buy that hanging drying thing. So simple.

Place the tomatoes, cut side up, on your rack (or whatever set up you've gone with) and leave them out in the sun until they are as dried as you like. Semi-dried gives you a much softer and brighter tomato flavour, while fully drying them results in a deep dark tomato flavour bomb, which can also be kept in the pantry for winter. Drying will take anything from 2–5 days, so just look in on them at the end of each day and stop the process when you've got them where you want them.

Now, this is going to sound really obvious, but I'll say it anyway so you don't send in hate mail: keep an eye on the weather report! If there is rain in your future, be sure to bring them inside or at least undercover. And put them back in the sun when she's shining.

Oven method

Preheat the oven to 110°C (230°F). Line a baking tray with baking paper, or top with a cooling rack.

Arrange the tomatoes, cut side up, on the paper or rack. Sprinkle very lightly with salt flakes.

Bake for 3 hours, then remove from the oven and gently press down on the tomatoes with a spatula to help release some of the excess moisture.

Return to the oven and bake for at least another 2 hours, or until dried to your taste.

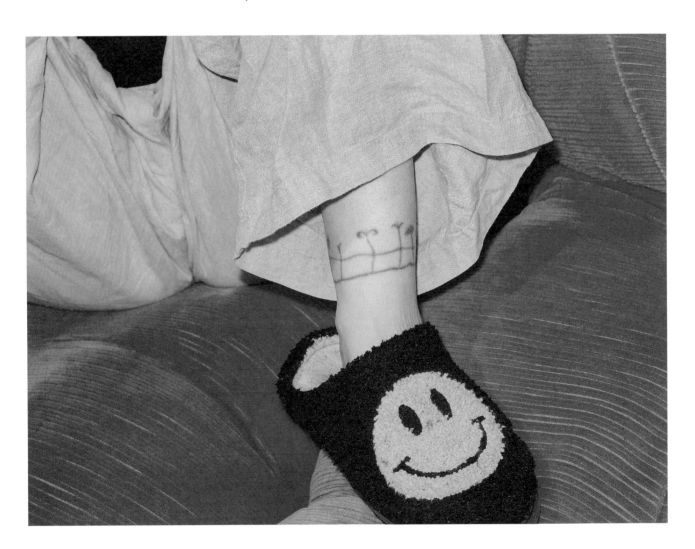

ARANCINI

Ever overcooked your rice? Got leftover risotto in the fridge? This is perfect for you. Feel free to fold in any leftovers. These also freeze well for when unexpected guests drop by.

Risotto

2 tablespoons extra-virgin olive oil

400 g (14 oz) arborio rice

125 ml (4 fl oz/½ cup) white wine

1 litre (34 fl oz/4 cups) vegan chicken or vegetable stock

50 g (1¾ oz/½ cup) grated vegan parmesan

40 g (1½ oz) vegan butter

1 teaspoon salt

cracked black pepper, to taste

Filling suggestions

vegan cubed mozzarella or other vegan cheese

vegan bolognese

vegan pesto

Crumb

150 g (5½ oz/1 cup) plain (all-purpose) flour

220 ml (7½ fl oz) soy milk

½ teaspoon salt

cracked black pepper, to taste

300 g (10½ oz/3 cups) dried breadcrumbs

vegetable oil, for deep-frying

salt flakes, to season

While arancini is the perfect way to use up left over risotto, this recipe is for those of you making it from scratch.

Heat the oil in a large, heavy-based saucepan over a medium heat, then add the rice. Stir well to coat in the oil, then pour in the wine. Cook until reduced by half, then pour in all the stock. Bring to the boil, then cover the pot and reduce the heat to a gentle simmer.

After about 15 minutes, check the rice. The liquid should be fully absorbed. If not, continue cooking for a few more minutes until tender. Once cooked, add the cheese, butter, salt and cracked black pepper, and stir well to combine. The rice should be soft and slightly sticky.

Spoon the rice onto a large plate or tray, then cover the surface with plastic wrap and refrigerate until cold. This can be done a day in advance.

Divide the rice into however many arancini you want to make. Roll into small balls for canapé (this is how you'll get thirty of them) or roll the mixture into equal portions for a main meal.

Fill a small bowl with water and keep it nearby so you can keep your hands wet while shaping the arancini. This will stop the rice sticking to your hands and make them much easier to shape.

Place a portion of the rice in the palm of your hand and flatten it out. Place the filling of your choice in the centre, then slowly start wrapping the rice around the filling, shaping it into a point towards your fingertips.

Once the filling is completely surrounded by the rice, sit the cone on a plate and push down slightly to create a flat bottom. Shape the remaining rice and filling.

For the crumb, whisk the flour and soy milk in a bowl until you have a smooth paste. Season with the salt and cracked black pepper. Pour the breadcrumbs into another bowl. Dip the arancini first in the batter, making sure they are completely coated, then dip in the breadcrumbs and coat well. At this point they can be frozen, refrigerated or cooked immediately.

Heat enough oil for deep-frying in a large stockpot or deep-fryer until it reaches 170°C (340°F). Gently lower the arancini into the oil and fry until golden brown all over. Remove and drain on paper towel. Season with a good pinch of salt flakes.

PICKLED MUSHROOMS

1 kg (2 lb 3 oz) mushrooms of your
    choice (see Note)

250 ml (8½ fl oz/1 cup) extra-virgin
    olive oil

250 ml (8½ fl oz/1 cup) red- or
    white-wine vinegar (I prefer red)

3 shallots, finely diced

4 garlic cloves, finely grated

zest of 1 lemon

zest of 1 orange

10 g (¼ oz/⅓ cup) fresh oregano leaves

2 thyme sprigs, leaves picked

½ teaspoon chilli flakes

1 teaspoon fennel seeds, crushed

2 bay leaves, torn

You can make this any time of the year. If you're lucky enough to live in a place where wild mushroom picking is accessible and you know what's safe to forage, then this just got a little bit extra. Either way, it's a win-win situation. I always make quite a large batch, as they keep in the fridge for a decent amount of time.

Bring a saucepan of heavily salted water to the boil over a high heat.

While the water is heating, sort through your mushrooms and decide on your preferred size. If you have small buttons, they look great on a platter if they're kept whole, but if you find yourself with fairly large mushrooms – especially if you've managed to forage some wild ones – you'll want to either cut them in half or even into thick slices.

Add the mushrooms to the boiling water and cook just until tender, about 5 minutes.

Drain in a colander then pat dry with a clean tea (dish) towel or paper towels.

In a large mixing bowl, combine the remaining ingredients and season well with salt and pepper.

Once the mushrooms are mostly dry, add them to the marinade and stir to coat.

Store the mushrooms in an airtight container and place in the fridge. Leave to marinate for at least 12 hours and be sure to bring them to room temperature before you serve them.

In the fridge, these could be stored for up to 3 months. Make sure the mushrooms are always submerged in the pickling liquid.

Note

You can use any meaty variety of mushroom you like. Button, Swiss, pine, shiitake and porcini (if you're lucky) are all suitable for pickling. Stay away from the delicate varieties like oyster mushrooms as they just get smooshy and you'll lose that satisfying bite you're after.

BRUSCHETTA

Broccoli

broccoli

garlic

chilli flakes

lemon

mint

Classic

heirloom tomato

red onion

garlic

basil

balsamic

Peach and ricotta

fresh peaches

Ricotta (page 23)

Pickled radicchio (page 30)

marjoram

Rapa and cannellini

braised rapa

mashed cannellini beans

Mushroom, chilli and mascarpone

Pickled mushrooms (page 40)

garlic

chilli flakes

thyme leaves

Mascarpone (page 24)

There are really no recipes for bruschetta. That being said, here are mine. Even if you haven't gone to the shops, as long as you have an old loaf of bread hanging around, you can make this. I purposefully haven't given you recipes here; more suggested flavour combinations and it is up to you how you prepare the ingredients. This is the perfect time to use leftovers and anything in those jars at the back of the fridge.

Slice your bread 1–2 cm (½–¾ in) thick, brush with olive oil and either toast in a frying pan or, even better, on a grill before adding your toppings of choice. Finish each with a drizzle of extra-virgin olive oil and a good crack of salt and pepper.

FRITTO MISTO

400 g (14 oz) king oyster mushrooms

400 g (14 oz) enoki mushrooms

vegetable oil, for deep-frying

salt flakes, for sprinkling

lemon wedges, to serve

Kombu broth

1 litre (34 fl oz/4 cups) water

10 × 15 cm (4 × 6 in) piece dried kombu, cut into thirds

15 g (½ oz) dried wakame

50 ml (1¾ fl oz) vegan fish sauce

1 tablespoon mushroom seasoning (optional; you can find this at most Asian grocery stores)

Batter

150 g (5½ oz) rice flour

60 g (2 oz) cornflour (cornstarch)

1 teaspoon baking powder

1 teaspoon salt

½ teaspoon freshly cracked black pepper

1 teaspoon sweet paprika

150 ml (5 fl oz) white wine

150 ml (5 fl oz) iced water

As a vegan, you probably haven't eaten a fritto misto in a while as it's usually made from a selection of fried seafood. Here, I give mushrooms an oceanic flavour by blanching them in kombu. Also, fried shit, f*ck yeah!

To prepare the king oyster mushrooms, start by trimming the end of the stalk then cutting off the caps. Slice the caps in half and shred the thick stalk into rough 1 cm (½ in) thick strips. For the enoki, trim off the woody end and break into small clusters about 2 cm (¾ in) thick. Place the prepared mushrooms in a large bowl.

For the kombu broth, add all the ingredients to a saucepan and bring to the boil. Reduce the heat to low and simmer for another 5 minutes, then turn off the heat.

Place a fine-mesh sieve over the mushrooms and pour the hot kombu broth over them. Allow the mushrooms to steep in the broth for a minimum of 30 minutes, or up to 2 hours.

To make the batter, add the rice flour, cornflour, baking powder, salt, pepper and paprika to a bowl and whisk to combine. Create a well in the centre of the flour mixture and pour in the wine and iced water, whisking continuously until the batter is smooth. It should resemble a thin pancake batter.

Heat about 5 cm (2 in) oil in a large saucepan or high-sided frying pan until it reaches 170°C (340°F).

Remove the mushrooms from the kombu broth and dry well with paper towel.

Working in batches, dip the mushrooms into the batter, making sure each piece is well coated, then drop into the oil and fry till golden brown and crispy.

Season with salt flakes and serve with lemon wedges.

OLIVE ASCOLANE (FRIED STUFFED OLIVES)

300 g (10½ oz) vegan feta cheese

100 g (3½ oz) vegan cream cheese

juice of ½ lemon

50 large green pitted olives (approx. 350 g/12½ oz)

150 g (5½ oz/1 cup) plain (all-purpose) flour

250 ml (8½ fl oz/1 cup) soy milk

2 tablespoons apple-cider vinegar or lemon juice

300 g (10½ oz/3 cups) fine breadcrumbs

vegetable oil, for deep-frying

I'm giving you a decent-sized recipe here because this recipe isn't hard, just a bit fiddly. So, my theory is if I'm going to go to the trouble of setting up a crumbing station and getting out a piping (pastry) bag, I may as well go to town and make a batch. The bonus is they freeze well, so future you will love you for it. Use whatever cheese you love and can get hold of for these – you don't even need to stuff them with cheese. They can be stuffed with seasoned, vegan ground (minced) beef, Sun-dried tomatoes (page 36), pesto – the options are endless. The version in this recipe is the one I serve at my venues. Now, you can replicate them at home.

Crumble the feta into the bowl of a stand mixer, then add the cream cheese, lemon juice and salt and pepper to taste. Beat with the paddle attachment until well combined and smooth.

The easiest way to stuff the olives is with a piping (pastry) bag. But if you don't have one, you can fill a resealable bag and cut off one of the corners. And if you don't have resealable bags, prepare to get messy and just stuff it in with your fingers. (Very clean fingers, obviously.) Pipe (or stuff) the filling into the olives.

Set up your crumbing station. You'll need three bowls or deep plates. In the first bowl, add the flour and mix in a little salt and pepper. In the second bowl mix together the soy milk and vinegar. Stir and allow to thicken for a few minutes. To the third bowl, add your breadcrumbs.

To crumb the olives, work in batches of five at a time. First, dust the olives in the flour, then dip into the soy-milk mixture and finish with a solid coating of breadcrumbs.

Once you've crumbed all the olives, refrigerate for 30 minutes to allow the cheese to firm up and the coating to set.

Heat enough oil for deep-frying in a large saucepan until it reaches 160°C (320°F).

Gently drop some of the olives into the oil and fry until golden brown. Be sure not to crowd the pan as this will drop the temperature of the oil and make the final product soggy and oily.

As they become golden, remove from the oil with a slotted spoon and drain on paper towel. Continue until all the olives have been fried. If you're a salt fiend like me, add some salt flakes to finish.

GIARDINIERA

These perfect Italian mixed pickles can be eaten on their own, put through a salad or chopped up in a sandwich. It is always good to have a jar of this in the fridge.

1 small or ½ medium cauliflower (approx. 500 g/1 lb 2 oz), cut into bite-sized florets

2 carrots (approx. 350 g/12½ oz), peeled and cut on an angle into 5 mm (¼ in) thick slices

3 celery stalks, cut on an angle into 5 mm (¼ in) thick slices

5 small pickling onions, peeled and quartered

1 fennel bulb, halved, core removed and sliced into 2 cm (¾ in) rectangles

1 red capsicum (bell pepper), sliced into 1 cm (½ in) thick strips

1 yellow capsicum (bell pepper), sliced into 1 cm (½ in) thick strips

500 ml (17 fl oz/2 cups) white-wine vinegar

500 ml (17 fl oz/2 cups) white vinegar

500 ml (17 fl oz/2 cups) water

40 g (1½ oz) fine salt

60 g (2 oz) caster (superfine) sugar

10 whole black peppercorns

1 teaspoon chilli flakes, or to taste

4 garlic cloves, peeled and smashed

6 juniper berries

3 thyme sprigs

2 bay leaves

Sterilise six 500 ml (17 fl oz/2 cups) or three 1 litre (34 fl oz/4 cups) jars.

Mix all the vegetables in a large bowl.

Add the remaining ingredients to a large stockpot and bring to the boil over a medium–high heat.

Add all the vegetables to the pot and stir to mix through. Cover with a lid and bring back to the boil. Once boiling, remove from the heat and use a slotted spoon to remove the vegetables from the pot and place back in the bowl. Strain the pickle solution into a jug.

Pack the vegetables into the jars and pour the hot brine over them, leaving a 1 cm (½ in) gap at the top.

Tap the jars on the bench a few times to remove any air bubbles, then screw the lids on tightly.

Rinse out the stockpot and place the jars in it. Fill with enough water to submerge the jars. Bring to the boil, then reduce the heat slightly and simmer for 10 minutes. Remove from the heat and allow to cool to room temperature.

Allow the pickle to sit for at least 3 days before eating. Properly sealed, the pickles will last at least 1 year in the pantry. Once opened, store in the fridge for up to 6 months, ensuring the vegetables stay submerged in the pickling liquid.

Do you know what really grinds my gears? Bottled dressings, sauces and jams. More often than not, they're full of preservatives and stabilisers, come in plastic, don't taste any good and are really expensive. There is nothing more disappointing than buying a beautiful head of radicchio, only to drown it in sad salad dressing.

This chapter will empower you to make your own vinaigrettes, jams, sauces and even a vegan version of Italy's most popular choc-hazelnut spread. Once you master these flavour bombs, you'll be able to turn any forgotten vegetable in your crisper, piece of bread or bag of dry pasta into a decent meal.

CONDIMENTI

25 g (1 oz) vegan belacan
(shrimp paste)

25 ml (¾ fl oz) vegan fish sauce

½ tablespoon white miso paste

50 g (1¾ oz) confit garlic cloves

1 garlic clove, peeled

100 ml (3½ fl oz) confit garlic oil

25 g (1 oz) vegan butter

50 ml (1¾ fl oz) vegan cream

BAGNA CAUDA

This one was a real hit-or-miss dish at the restaurant. I learned that you have to really appreciate punchy flavours to appreciate this. If you don't like salty, funky flavours, move along.

Add the belacan, fish sauce, miso paste, confit and raw garlic to a blender or food processor and blitz to combine. With the motor running, slowly drizzle in the oil until the mixture is smooth.

When you're ready to serve, melt the butter in a saucepan over a low heat and add the paste. Cook for about 3 minutes, then return the paste to the blender and, with the motor running, slowly add the cream. Blend on high speed until emulsified. If it's not coming together, try slowly adding water until incorporated.

Serve with crudités and boiled new potatoes. If you have any left over, store in an airtight container in the fridge for up to 4 days.

CALABRIAN CHILLI PASTE

4 shallots, roughly chopped

10 garlic cloves, chopped

50 g (1¾ oz) capers in brine, drained

100 g (3½ oz) red chillies, destemmed (to taste; see Note)

300 g (10½ oz) eggplant (aubergine), peeled and roughly chopped

200 g (7 oz) button mushrooms, roughly chopped

500 g (1 lb 2 oz) red capsicum (bell pepper), deseeded and roughly chopped

250 ml (8½ fl oz/1 cup) extra-virgin olive oil

50 ml (1¾ fl oz) vegan fish sauce (optional)

2 teaspoons fennel seeds, crushed

1 teaspoon dried oregano

100 ml (3½ fl oz) red-wine vinegar

It is the bomb, literally. If you can't handle spice, why are you even reading this page? It's enough to make your eyes water.

To a food processor, add the shallot, garlic, capers and chillies. Pulse until finely chopped, but not quite a paste. Scrape into a bowl.

Add the eggplant and mushroom to the food processor and pulse until finely minced, then place in another bowl.

Finally, add the capsicum to the food processor and pulse until finely minced.

Heat 50 ml (1¾ fl oz) of the olive oil in a heavy, shallow dutch oven over a medium heat. Add the shallot, garlic, caper and chilli mixture, along with a large pinch of salt, and cook for 2–3 minutes, or until beginning to soften.

Next, add the eggplant and mushroom with another large pinch of salt and fry for another 5 minutes, or until the eggplant begins to collapse.

If using, pour the fish sauce in, then add the fennel seeds and oregano.

Add the capsicum to the pan and stir well to combine. Cook over a medium–low heat for 30 minutes, stirring regularly until most of the moisture has been cooked out and you have a fairly thick mixture.

Pour in the vinegar, stir well, then take off the heat.

Stir in the remaining olive oil and season to taste. Add to a container and top with a little more oil if necessary to submerge the paste. Seal and store in the fridge for up to 1 month.

Note

Technically you should be using Calabrian chillies. If you're lucky, you'll be able to find them either jarred or dried in a good Italian grocer. If you find dried, be sure to rehydrate them in water before using. But please, if you don't have access to them, use whatever red chillies are available to you.

1 nori sheet
60 ml (2 fl oz/¼ cup) vegan fish sauce
20 g (¾ oz) capers in brine, drained
1 tablespoon dijon mustard
60 ml (2 fl oz/¼ cup) soy milk
juice of ½ lemon
1 teaspoon sugar
150 ml (5 fl oz) extra-virgin olive oil

ANCHOVY DRESSING

Another recipe that is great on everything! One of my favourite ways to eat this is poured over boiled potatoes. Just make sure you buy great quality potatoes from a grower and not the supermarket. The difference is night and day. Trust me.

Toast the nori sheet over an open flame or in a dry frying pan until toasted brown spots appear.

Add all the ingredients, except the olive oil, to a blender. Blitz on medium speed until well combined.

With the motor running, slowly drizzle in the oil until fully emulsified. Season to taste with salt and pepper.

Store in a sealed container for up to 1 week.

zest and juice of 1 blood orange
    (approx. 70 ml/2¼ fl oz), or you can
    use regular orange juice
1 tablespoon dijon mustard
30 ml (1 fl oz) balsamic vinegar
1 tablespoon brown sugar
1 garlic clove, finely grated
1 teaspoon salt flakes
¼ teaspoon ground fennel
ground black pepper, to taste
125 ml (4 fl oz/½ cup) extra-virgin
    olive oil

BLOOD ORANGE & BALSAMIC DRESSING

If you don't have a blender, you can also make this dressing in a jar with a tight-fitting lid. Just throw everything in and shake for dear life.

Add all the ingredients, except the olive oil, to a blender and blitz until well combined.

With the motor running, slowly incorporate the oil until emulsified. Season to taste.

Store in the fridge for up to 1 week.

CREAMY OLIVE VINAIGRETTE

150 g (5½ oz) large green pitted olives
1 small garlic clove, peeled
1 teaspoon dijon mustard
40 ml (1¼ fl oz) lemon juice
4 tarragon sprigs, leaves picked and finely chopped
60 ml (2 fl oz/¼ cup) extra-virgin olive oil

This is just another delicious sauce to throw on food, unless you don't like olives. In which case, you're wrong.

Place the olives and garlic into a mortar and pestle and grind to a thick paste. Transfer to a bowl. (If you don't have a mortar and pestle, you can either blitz in a blender or food processor, or simple chop by hand until you have a chunky paste.)

Add the dijon, lemon juice and tarragon to the paste and stir in to combine.

Slowly add the olive oil, stirring constantly, then season to taste.

Store in airtight container for up to 2 weeks.

TOMATO VINAIGRETTE

350 g (12½ oz) fresh tomatoes, grated
2 tablespoons sherry vinegar
100 ml (3½ fl oz) extra-virgin olive oil
1 garlic clove, finely grated
1 teaspoon caster (superfine) sugar
pinch of dried oregano

If the title of this recipe isn't doing it for you, I can't help you. It's just perfect. It's even good for just dipping your bread in. When I was little, my brother and I used to fight over the juice in the bowl when the salad was finished. This is *that*.

In a small bowl, whisk all the ingredients together and allow to stand for 30 minutes.

When ready to serve, pour into a jar and shake like crazy, then pour immediately.

Store left over vinaigrette in the fridge for up to 5 days.

PESTO TRAPANESE

**MAKES APPROX.
500 G (1 LB 2 OZ)**

2 large garlic cloves, peeled

1 teaspoon salt flakes

50 g (1¾ oz) blanched almonds, toasted

1 large bunch of basil, leaves picked

6 mint leaves

300 g (10½ oz) Sun-dried tomatoes (page 36), or fresh tomatoes

100 ml (3½ fl oz) extra-virgin olive oil

50 g (1¾ oz/½ cup) grated vegan parmesan

1 teaspoon red-wine vinegar

Traditionally, this is made with fresh tomatoes in summer. In winter, basil is grown hydroponically which makes the leaves thin and flaccid. But, if the cravings are real, you can make this with the preserved, Sun-dried (page 36) or Smoked tomatoes (page 19) to make up for the under-performing basil. Are we still talking about pesto, here?

Add the garlic, salt and almonds to a blender or food processor and pulse until roughly chopped.

Add the basil, mint, tomatoes, olive oil and parmesan and blend to a rough paste. Make sure it remains slightly chunky. Season to taste with red-wine vinegar, salt and pepper.

Drizzle a little olive oil on top and store in an airtight container in the fridge for up to 2 weeks.

TRADITIONAL PESTO

MAKES 300 G (10½ OZ)

1 garlic clove, peeled

1 teaspoon salt flakes

40 g (1½ oz/¼ cup) pine nuts, toasted (see Note)

1 large bunch of basil, leaves picked (approx. 80 g/2¾ oz, firmly packed)

125 ml (4 fl oz/½ cup) extra-virgin olive oil

25 g (1 oz/¼ cup) grated vegan parmesan

Note
For a nut-free version, swap the pine nuts with toasted pepitas (pumpkin seeds) or sunflower seeds.

If you are short on time or don't have a mortar and pestle, add all the ingredients to a blender and blitz until smooth. Make sure not to over-blend, as you don't want to heat up the basil.

If you have a mortar and pestle, I recommend that you take the extra few minutes and make your pesto in it. The final result is just a little more lush.

Start by adding the garlic and salt to the mortar and crush to a fine paste. Add the pine nuts and continue to crush until they are finely ground.

Slowly start adding the basil leaves, one handful at a time. Crush the leaves then gradually incorporate some oil. Repeat this process until all the basil and oil have been used.

Using the pestle, stir through the parmesan and check and adjust the seasoning.

Drizzle a little olive oil on top and store in an airtight container in the fridge for up to 2 weeks.

AGRODOLCE SAUCE

80 ml (2½ fl oz/⅓ cup) extra-virgin olive oil

1 red capsicum (bell pepper), deseeded and thinly sliced

1 red onion, thinly sliced

3 garlic cloves, finely minced

1 teaspoon fennel seeds

1 long red chilli, thinly sliced

100 g (3½ oz) sultanas or raisins

140 ml (4½ fl oz) red-wine vinegar

80 g (2¾ oz/⅓ cup) caster (superfine) sugar

500 g (1 lb 2 oz) Passata (page 16)

150 g (5½ oz) caperberries, stalks removed and thinly sliced

large handful of parsley

Who doesn't like sweet and sour? It is plain sexy. This is a great dressing to throw on any grilled vegetable to amp up the flavour. Boom, you've got yourself a perfect side dish.

In a deep frying pan, heat the oil over a low heat, then add the sliced capsicum and onion with a large pinch of salt and sauté for about 10 minutes, stirring often until soft. Add the garlic and continue to cook for a further 2 minutes.

Next, add the fennel seeds, chilli, sultanas, vinegar and sugar. Cook down for a few minutes until the sugar begins to melt and slightly caramelise, then add the passata. Season well with salt and pepper and slowly reduce over a low heat until very thick, stirring every 5 minutes or so. This will take about 20 minutes.

Add the sliced caperberries and parsley and stir to combine.

Store in a jar, topped with olive oil in the fridge for up to 1 month.

GREMOLATA

1 bunch of parsley, leaves picked and finely chopped

½ bunch of mint, leaves picked and finely chopped

2 garlic cloves, finely grated

zest of 1 lemon

1 tablespoon capers in brine, drained and finely chopped

pinch of chilli flakes (optional)

It may seem like a lot of chopping but it is worth it. Plus, you can put gremolata on almost anything. Chop, chop!

Combine all the ingredients in a bowl and whisk well to combine.

Allow to stand at room temperature for 30 minutes before using.

This is best used straight away. Any leftovers can be covered in olive oil and stored in the fridge for up to 1 week.

PANGRATTATO

MAKES 300 G (10½ OZ)

250 g (9 oz) stale bread, crusts removed

100 ml (3½ fl oz) extra-virgin olive oil

2 garlic cloves, peeled and smashed

½ bunch of parsley, very finely chopped

4 thyme sprigs, leaves stripped and finely chopped

zest of ½ lemon

I cannot stand food waste. Pangrattato is a great way to use up bread that is a little past its prime while adding flavour and texture to your food. They don't call it poor man's parmesan for nuthin'.

Using a food processor, blitz the bread in batches to break it down into fine crumbs.

Heat the olive oil in a large frying pan over a low heat along with the smashed garlic cloves. Cook until the garlic is golden brown and has infused the oil, then remove the garlic from the pan.

Add the breadcrumbs, chopped herbs and lemon zest to the pan and stir well to evenly coat in the oil. Season well.

Cook over a low heat, stirring regularly, until the bread begins to turn a deep golden colour and is nice and dry, about 10–15 minutes.

In an airtight container, this can be stored in the fridge for up to 1 week.

PRICKLY PEAR JAM

MAKES APPROX. 400 G (14 OZ)

700 g (1 lb 9 oz) prickly pears (peeled weight will be approx. 550 g/1 lb 3 oz)

300 g (10½ oz) caster (superfine) sugar

juice of 1 lemon

Outside of Mexico, Italy is the largest consumer of prickly pears. Unlike Mexicans, Italians don't actually eat the cactus paddle. WARNING: the spikes will F*CK you up. Even if you buy them from the grocers, there will be some spikes remaining, so handle with caution. I recommend handling them with a flamethrower.

Place the prickly pears in a blender and blitz on high speed to create a puree, breaking the large seeds into very small pieces. This will take a few minutes.

Pour the prickly pear puree into a stainless steel or enamel saucepan and add the sugar and lemon juice. Stir to combine.

Bring to the boil, then reduce the heat to low and simmer for 20–30 minutes.

To test that the jam is ready, dip a cold spoon into the jam. Once ready, the jam should fall off the spoon in a thick drop when lifted. If it drips off the spoon too quickly, continue to cook until the drops are thick.

Seal well and store in the fridge for up to 6 months, or can it if you're confident in your preserving skills and keep in the pantry.

FIG JAM

1 kg (2 lb 3 oz) fresh figs, each cut into eight pieces
200 g (7 oz) caster (superfine) sugar
40 ml (1¼ fl oz) lemon juice
1 bay leaf
150 ml (5 fl oz) water

This jam can be made either cheap or almost free. Cheap is when you go to the market when figs are in season and buy them by the tray. Free is when you find out where all the wogs live and scavenge the overhanging fruit from the trees. Remember anything over the fence is free game. Pair it with sweet or savoury dishes.

Sterilise two 500 ml (17 fl oz/2 cups) jars.

Add the cut figs and sugar to a large, heavy-based stainless steel or enamel saucepan. Stir well, then leave to stand for 30 minutes, stirring occasionally to allow the sugar to dissolve and start breaking down the figs.

Add the lemon juice, bay leaf and water and bring to the boil over a high heat.

Reduce the heat to low and simmer gently until the fruit is soft and the liquid is very thick. Stir often to ensure it doesn't stick to the bottom of the pot. This will take between 30–40 minutes.

To test that it's ready, chill a small plate in the freezer while the jam is cooking. Start testing at the 30-minute mark by placing a small amount of jam onto the chilled plate. If the jam holds its shape when you tilt the plate, it's ready.

Remove the bay leaf and pour the warm jam into the clean, sterilised jars. Seal well and store in the fridge for up to 6 months.

250 g (9 oz) raw hazelnuts

40 g (1½ oz) vegan dark chocolate chips

1 teaspoon vanilla paste or extract

20 g (¾ oz) dark cocoa powder

80 g (2¾ oz) icing (confectioners') sugar

1 teaspoon salt flakes

30 g (1 oz) refined coconut oil, melted

NOT-NUTELLA

Is the OG delicious? Yes. Is it vegan? Definitely not. This version is, and it also cuts out the food miles. You have the right to feel smug while slathering this on your toast. Your conscience is clear.

Preheat the oven to 180°C (360°F).

Place the hazelnuts on a baking tray lined with baking paper and bake for 10 minutes. Remove from the oven and leave to cool for a few minutes then place in a clean tea (dish) towel. Gather up the corners of the towel to make a pouch, then rub the hazelnuts to remove as much of the skins as possible.

Add the hazelnuts to a food processor and blitz until they turn into a smooth butter. This can take up to 10 minutes, so every few minutes, stop the motor and scrape down the sides.

Once you have a very smooth hazelnut butter add the chocolate chips and blend for another 2 minutes, or until the chocolate has melted through the hazelnut butter, then add the remaining ingredients. Blend for a final minute to combine all the ingredients and check the flavour. If you prefer it sweeter, feel free to add more sugar.

At this point the texture will be runny, so pour it into a jar or container and refrigerate it until thickened.

Store in the fridge for up to 1 month.

Do not underestimate a stellar support act. Just remember, The Cure once played support, too. The salads and sides in this chapter are a great accompaniment to the mains, breads and pastas in the other chapters, but you know what, they can also stand alone.

I am very passionate about a properly dressed salad because I've been served too many sopping wet, overdressed leaves, or bone-dry ones. If there is anything you take away from this chapter, please let it be how to dress your greens. Once you make a perfect salad, you'll find them very easy to eat.

As for the side dishes, they don't always have to be sides. I've spent many afternoons grazing on braised vegetables, or eating spoonfuls of beans, realising that I have made a meal out of them. In fact, the fava bean and chicory recipe on page 88 inadvertently became my dinner one night while I was writing this book. Just remember, they're only support acts if you keep them from the main stage.

INSALATE & CONTORNI

ROMAN-STYLE ARTICHOKES

1 lemon, zest removed then cut in half

½ teaspoon fennel seeds, crushed

30 g (1 oz/½ cup) finely chopped parsley

15 g (½ oz/¼ cup) finely chopped mint

7 g (¼ oz/¼ cup) finely chopped oregano

4 garlic cloves, finely minced

125 ml (4 fl oz/½ cup) extra-virgin olive oil, plus extra for drizzling

4 large globe artichokes or 8 small artichokes, cleaned (see page 33)

125 ml (4 fl oz/½ cup) white wine

salt flakes, to serve

This is a quintessential Italian dish. It would be rude not to include it.

In a small bowl, stir together the lemon zest, fennel seeds, parsley, mint, oregano, garlic, 60 ml (2 fl oz/¼ cup) of the olive oil and season well.

Pack the herb mixture between the leaves of the prepped artichokes and over the cut surface.

Pour the remaining olive oil into a pot that will tightly fit the artichokes, so they remain in place while cooking. Pack in the artichokes, cut side down, and place the pot over a medium–high heat. Fry for 1 minute before adding the wine, then cook for a further minute to cook off the alcohol before adding enough water to come halfway up the artichokes. Season well.

Bring up to the boil, then reduce the heat to low and cover with a lid. Cook for 20–30 minutes depending on the size of the artichokes.

The artichokes are done when a sharp knife can be easily pushed through the base of the artichoke.

To serve, gently remove the artichokes from the pot and serve, cut side down, on a plate. Drizzle with some extra olive oil and salt flakes. Serve warm or at room temperature.

RADICCHIO & BEETROOT SALAD

4 beetroots (beets), scrubbed

2 tablespoons extra-virgin olive oil

3 thyme sprigs

150 ml (5 fl oz) Blood orange and
    balsamic dressing (page 56)

1 head radicchio, quartered,
    core removed

1 fennel, halved, core removed,
    finely sliced

½ bunch of parsley, leaves picked

This is a really visually appealing and tasty salad. It's a fantastic addition to a large spread.

Preheat the oven to 200°C (390°F).

Rub the beetroots with the oil and some salt, then loosely wrap together in foil with the thyme sprigs. Bake for about 1 hour, or until a sharp knife can be pushed through a beetroot without much resistance.

While the beetroots are still warm, rub off the skins, then cut into rough wedges. Place in a large bowl and pour the dressing over the top. Toss well to coat.

Tear the radicchio wedges into uneven pieces and add to the beetroot.

Add the fennel to the bowl, along with the picked parsley leaves. Season with salt and pepper and toss well to coat.

CHICORY SALAD

500 g (1 lb 2 oz) chicory (endive) or
  puntarelle, tough stalks removed
  and shredded into thin strips.
  (If using frisee, just remove the base
  and separate the leaves. Shred any
  extra-large leaves.)
¼ bunch of parsley, finely chopped
150–200 ml (5–7 fl oz) Anchovy
  dressing (page 56)

If you want a sweeter salad, buy small chicory (endive). If you
think bitter greens are the best thing on earth, buy big chicory.
No prizes for guessing which one I go with.

If you can get your hands on puntarelle – a type of chicory that's grown
in winter – then use it! If not, use whatever form of chicory you can find.
This includes endive and frisee (all types of chicory). As long as it's bitter,
you're good.

Place the shredded chicory in a bowl of iced water and allow to firm
up and curl for 30–60 minutes. This will also help remove some of
the bitterness.

Once the chicory has soaked, drain and dry well in a salad spinner or
tea (dish) towel.

Transfer to a bowl, add the parsley and pour the dressing over the top.
Toss well to mix and season to taste. This salad needs to be quite heavily
dressed, so be liberal with the dressing. Serve immediately.

SERVES 4

BRAISED FENNEL

40 g (1½ oz) vegan butter
2 tablespoons extra-virgin olive oil
6 shallots, thinly sliced
1 head garlic, cut through the middle
4 fennel bulbs, or 12 baby fennel
150 ml (5 fl oz) white wine
400 ml (13½ fl oz) vegan chicken or
  vegetable stock
6 marjoram or oregano sprigs
juice and zest of ½ lemon
¼ bunch of parsley, roughly chopped

It annoys me how many people say they don't like fennel.
This recipe will convert them.

Heat the butter and oil in a large, heavy-based frying pan or shallow
dutch oven over a medium–low heat. Add the shallot and garlic, cut side
down, season well and cook for about 5 minutes, or until softened and
lightly golden.

Add the fennel, wine, stock and marjoram, and season again. Bring to the
boil, stirring gently to coat the fennel in the liquid, then reduce the heat
to low and cover. Braise the fennel until tender, about 20–40 minutes
depending on the size of the fennel. Flip the fennel once during cooking.

Once the fennel is cooked, lift it out and place on a serving dish. Press down
on the garlic to remove the softened cloves and roughly mash them with
a wooden spoon. Add the lemon juice and zest and simmer the remaining
liquid until it begins to thicken slightly, about 3 minutes. Stir the parsley in
and season well then pour this mixture over the fennel and serve.

ROASTED CHESTNUTS & LENTILS

60 ml (2 fl oz/¼ cup) extra-virgin olive oil

2 celery stalks, diced

1 small carrot, diced

1 brown onion, diced

6 garlic cloves, sliced

20 g (¾ oz) dried porcini mushrooms, soaked in boiling water for 30 minutes

250 g (9 oz) black lentils

200 g (7 oz) roasted chestnuts, roughly chopped

1 bay leaf

1 rosemary sprig

1 thyme sprig

125 ml (4 fl oz/½ cup) red wine

300 ml (10 fl oz) porcini soaking liquid

300 ml (10 fl oz) vegan chicken stock or water

handful of parsley, roughly chopped

To me, this is a hug in a bowl. It will warm you from the inside out. I don't recommend eating this for lunch unless you plan on napping for the rest of the day.

Heat the oil in a large frying pan over a medium heat. Once hot, add the celery, carrot and onion along with a pinch of salt and cook over a low heat for 3–4 minutes, or until nice and soft. Add the garlic and cook for another minute.

Remove the porcini from the soaking liquid (retain the liquid) and squeeze the mushrooms to remove any excess. Roughly chop and add to the vegetables. Stir to combine and cook for 1 minute.

Add the lentils, chestnuts, bay leaf, rosemary and thyme. Stir, then pour in the wine and cook out for a minute before adding the porcini soaking liquid and stock.

Season well then cover with a lid and cook for 30–40 minutes over a low heat, or until the lentils are cooked through but not falling apart. Stir through the parsley.

Serve with soft or fried polenta, or tossed through pasta. I recommend just buying a big loaf of bread and digging in.

POTATOES & PEPPERS

100 ml (3½ fl oz) extra-virgin olive oil

500 g (1 lb 2 oz) waxy potatoes, peeled and sliced into 2 cm (¾ in) thick rounds (if the potatoes are large, cut in half lengthways first)

2 whole dried chillies, bruised, or ½ teaspoon chilli flakes

125 ml (4 fl oz/½ cup) water

3 garlic cloves, thickly sliced

1 red capsicum (bell pepper), roasted, peeled and deseeded

1 green capsicum (bell pepper), roasted, peeled and deseeded

1 tablespoon red-wine vinegar

½ bunch of parsley, roughly chopped

This is one of the ultimate one-pot wonders. Serve this with the Fava bean puree (page 88) – these two dishes together are the GOAT.

Heat the oil in a large frying pan over a medium heat for 30 seconds, then add the sliced potato and dried chillies. Toss to coat in the oil, then add the water along with a large pinch of salt. Cover with a lid and cook for 5 minutes, then remove the lid and toss the potatoes.

Continue cooking uncovered until the water has evaporated and the potatoes are beginning to soften, about 5 minutes.

Turn the potatoes regularly until they are golden on both sides, then add the garlic, being careful to not break up the potatoes too much.

Tear the roasted capsicums roughly into 1 cm (½ in) strips and mix through the potatoes.

Pour the vinegar over the top, add the chopped parsley and season well with salt and pepper. Gently toss, then serve.

AGRODOLCE PEPPERS

60 ml (2 fl oz/¼ cup) extra-virgin
olive oil

1 large shallot, finely minced

2 garlic cloves, finely minced

60 g (2 oz/½ cup) sultanas or
golden raisins

juice and zest of ½ orange

30 g (1 oz) sugar or agave

200 ml (7 fl oz) red-wine vinegar

2 thyme sprigs

40 g (1½ oz) whole capers

1 tablespoon vegan fish sauce
(optional)

1 teaspoon salt flakes

freshly cracked black pepper

6 large capsicums (bell peppers;
all one colour or a mix),
roasted and peeled

50 g (1¾ oz) toasted pine nuts, to serve

This is the kind of thing I keep in my fridge and eat out of the jar while staring blankly at the shelves wondering what to have for dinner.

Heat the oil in a small saucepan over a medium heat. Add the shallot and garlic and cook for about 2 minutes, or until softened and lightly brown.

Add the remaining ingredients, except the peppers and pine nuts, and bring to the boil, then reduce the heat to low and simmer, stirring every few minutes until reduced by half and becoming slightly syrupy, about 15 minutes. Take off the heat and allow to cool to room temperature. Remove the thyme stalks and check the seasoning.

Tear the roasted peppers in thick strips and place in a bowl. Pour over the agrodolce dressing and allow to sit at room temperature for at least 1 hour before serving.

When you're ready to serve, pour onto a plate and garnish with the toasted pine nuts.

BRAISED RADICCHIO & PEAR

2 tablespoons extra-virgin olive oil,
    plus extra for drizzling

1 round head radicchio, cut into
    six wedges, core removed

2 pears, peeled, quartered and cored

200 ml (7 fl oz) vegetable stock

60 ml (2 fl oz/¼ cup) balsamic vinegar

4 thyme sprigs

½ teaspoon salt

freshly cracked black pepper, to taste

Yes, this is another radicchio recipe. Yes, I love it.

Preheat the oven to 200°C (390°F).

Heat the oil in a shallow enamel pan over a medium heat.

Add the radicchio and pear, cut side down, and cook for 2 minutes, or until beginning to brown. Flip and cook on the other cut side for another 2 minutes.

Pour the vegetable stock and balsamic vinegar over the top, then drop in the thyme sprigs and season with salt and pepper. Bring to the boil, then place in the oven and bake for 20–25 minutes, or until the pears are tender. Remove the thyme sprigs.

If your pan isn't oven safe, transfer the radicchio and pears to a ceramic baking tray and put to the side. Pour the remaining ingredients into the pan and bring to the boil, pour into the baking dish, then place in the oven to bake.

Serve with an extra drizzle of olive oil and seasoning.

BRAISED RAPA

SERVES 4

1 large bunch of rapa, tough ends
    removed

60 ml (2 fl oz/¼ cup) extra-virgin
    olive oil

3 garlic cloves, finely sliced

½–1 teaspoon chilli flakes

2 tablespoons vegan fish sauce
    (optional)

juice of ½ lemon

This might look like leafy broccoli, but it is not. It's another one of those ingredients that you don't get to eat often throughout the year. Grab them when you can.

Bring a large pot of heavily salted water to the boil.

Gather up the bunch of rapa and cut into three large lengths.

Blanch for 5 minutes, then pour into a colander over the sink and rinse under cold water. Squeeze out the excess moisture using your hands. Set aside.

Heat the olive oil in a large frying pan with the garlic and chilli flakes. Cook over a medium heat until the garlic turns a light golden brown, then add the rapa and fish sauce, if using. Toss to coat and cook over a medium–high heat for about 3 minutes. Add the lemon juice, season well, and toss once more to combine. Serve immediately.

Leftovers are great tossed through pasta.

POLENTA

Soft polenta

800 ml (27 fl oz) water, or vegan chicken or vegetable stock

450 ml (15 fl oz) soy milk, or more water or stock

1 teaspoon salt

160 g (5½ oz) polenta (not instant)

40 g (1½ oz) vegan butter

30 g (1 oz) vegan parmesan, grated (optional)

Firm polenta

1 litre (34 fl oz/4 cups) water, or vegan chicken or vegetable stock

160 g (5½ oz/1 cup) polenta (not instant)

olive oil, for greasing

Consider this your masterclass in making polenta. Once you can make these recipes, you will always be able to feed yourself on a dime. There is a basic ratio for polenta. If you're after a soft and creamy polenta, the ratio is one part polenta to five parts liquid. If you're after a firm polenta that you can hard-set to grill or fry, the ratio is one part polenta to four parts liquid. That being said, there are a lot of variables, including the type of polenta you use, and personal preference can play a big part in the final product. Use these ratios as a guide and you'll be on the right track. Instant polenta is very quick and easy to cook, but can result in a less texturally satisfying and tasty end product. It's still good, just not *as* good. So, if you have the time and patience to stir a pot for 30–40 minutes, stick with the original long-cooking polenta.

For the soft polenta, heat the water, soy milk and salt in a large, heavy-based saucepan. Bring to the boil, then turn down to a low simmer.

In a slow and steady stream, pour in the polenta, whisking constantly until fully incorporated.

Continue to cook for anywhere between 30–40 minutes. It will start very thin and, over time, become smooth and thick. If it becomes too hard to stir with a whisk, swap to a wooden spoon. If the polenta starts to become too thick before it is fully cooked, add a little extra liquid.

When soft and creamy, stir through the butter and parmesan, if using, and season well. Serve immediately.

To make firm polenta, bring the water to the boil in a saucepan over a high heat and add the polenta in a steady stream, whisking constantly until fully incorporated.

Continue to cook for anywhere between 30–40 minutes. It will start very thin and, over time, become quite thick. Season well with salt and pepper.

Once the polenta is cooked through and holds fairly well on a spoon, pour onto a greased tray and smooth out with a wet spatula. Allow to cool on the bench before covering with plastic wrap and refrigerating to fully set.

Once set, cut into desired shapes and grill or deep-fry.

GNOCCHI ALLA ROMANA

500 ml (17 fl oz/2 cups) soy milk

1 bay leaf

1 garlic clove, smashed

¼ brown onion, sliced

4 black peppercorns

500 ml (17 fl oz/2 cups) vegan chicken or vegetable stock

180 g (6½ oz) semolina flour (not instant)

100 g (3½ oz/1 cup) grated vegan parmesan, plus extra to serve (optional)

80 g (2¾ oz) vegan butter, plus extra for greasing

pinch of ground nutmeg

This is one of the most impressive, affordable side dishes you could ever make. It costs next to nothing and tastes like a million bucks. Now, what else do I have to say to convince you to make it?

Add the soy milk, bay leaf, garlic, onion and peppercorns to a small saucepan and bring to the boil over a high heat. Once boiling, remove from the heat and set aside to infuse for 15 minutes.

Strain the milk into a larger saucepan and add the stock. Bring back to the boil over a high heat, then reduce the heat to a low simmer.

Slowly add the semolina flour in a thin stream, whisking continuously. Cook the semolina for 15–20 minutes, or until the mixture becomes very thick and starts to pull away from the side of the pan. (When the semolina is too thick to whisk, switch to a wooden spoon.)

Remove from the heat and stir in the parmesan, half the butter and the nutmeg. Season heavily with salt and white pepper.

Spray a baking tray with oil and pour the semolina onto it, spreading it out into an even layer about 1.5 cm (½ in) thick. Leave to cool for about 30 minutes, or until it has completely set.

While the semolina is setting, preheat the oven to 200°C (390°F).

Grease the bottom and sides of a 2 litre (68 fl oz/8 cup) ovenproof baking dish with a little butter.

Using a round cutter or glass (roughly 5 cm/2 in in diameter), cut the semolina into discs, dipping the cutter in some water if it begins to stick between cuts.

Layer the semolina rounds into the greased baking dish, slightly overlapping. Dot with the remaining butter and lightly season the top with extra salt and pepper.

Bake, uncovered, for 20 minutes, or until a light golden crust forms on top, then remove from the oven and grate over a little extra parmesan if desired.

Allow to cool for a few minutes to allow it to slightly firm up before serving.

FAVA BEAN PUREE

This is my favourite dish ever. I could eat this every day, forever and ever and ever. While I would like you to follow the recipe for the puree, the vegetable you use to top it is up to you. I use chicory because I love bitter leaves, but you can use any seasonal green. Even zucchini is great here. Just follow the method. I don't want to see anything crunchy on this.

Fava bean puree

350 g (12½ oz) split fava (broad) beans
2 garlic cloves, peeled
1 bay leaf
150 g (5½ oz) potato, peeled and diced
1 teaspoon salt

Chicory

1 large bunch of chicory (endive), tough ends removed
50 ml (1¾ fl oz) extra-virgin olive oil, plus extra for drizzling
3 garlic cloves, finely sliced
½ teaspoon chilli flakes
2 tablespoons vegan fish sauce (optional)

Place the split fava beans, garlic cloves and bay leaf into a large saucepan and cover with 1.2 litres (41 fl oz) cold water. Bring to the boil over a high heat, then reduce the heat to low and simmer gently for 30 minutes. Remove any foam that floats to the surface with a slotted spoon or small strainer. Top up the water as necessary to keep the beans submerged.

After the 30 minutes, add the potato and continue simmering until the fava and potato have broken down to a mushy consistency. By this point the water should have almost completely absorbed. Stir often at this point to avoid the vegetables catching on the bottom of the pan.

Remove from the heat and beat the mixture with a wooden spoon until smooth. Season with salt and set aside.

Wash the chicory and cut into 5 cm (2 in) pieces. Bring a saucepan of water to the boil and cook the chicory for 10 minutes, stirring occasionally.

Pour into a colander over the sink and rinse the chicory under cold water. Drain, squeezing out the excess water with your hands.

Heat the oil in a large frying pan over a medium heat with the garlic and chilli flakes. Cook until the garlic turns a light golden brown, then add the chicory and fish sauce, if using. Toss to coat and continue cooking for about another 3 minutes. Season well.

To serve, place the fava puree back over a low heat and add a splash of water if needed to bring the mixture back to a smooth paste. It should have the consistency of runny mashed potatoes.

Pour the puree onto a large serving dish, then top with the cooked chicory and finish with a large drizzle of olive oil.

Note

Instead of chicory, you can use other bitter leaves such as endive, escarole, radicchio or dandelion leaves. Cut into 5 cm (2 in) pieces and add to boiling water for about 30 seconds or skip the boiling process altogether and just add raw greens to the frying pan.

CHARRED MELON & TOMATO PANZANELLA

300 g (10½ oz) stale bread, crusts removed and torn into rough 5 cm (2 in) pieces

50 ml (1¾ fl oz) extra-virgin olive oil

1 large garlic clove, finely grated

1 teaspoon salt flakes

½ cantaloupe, skin and seeds removed, cut into 5 cm (2 in) thick slices

500 g (1 lb 2 oz) mixed heirloom tomatoes, cored and roughly cut

20 g (¾ oz/1 cup) parsley, leaves picked

50 g (1¾ oz/1 cup) purple basil, leaves picked

Dressing

150 ml (5 fl oz) Tomato vinaigrette (page 57)

Panzanella is just a way to incorporate vegetables into your daily carb intake. It's another way to use up stale bread and make it taste better than it did to begin with.

Preheat the oven to 200°C (390°F).

Place the torn bread in a large bowl with the oil, grated garlic and salt flakes. Toss well with your hands to coat the bread, then place on a flat baking tray.

Bake until the bread is golden and crispy, stirring a few times to get an even colour – about 15 minutes. Remove and allow to cool.

Heat a barbecue chargrill or chargrill pan until hot and grill the melon slices until charred on both sides. Remove and cut into large chunks.

Add the tomatoes and melon to a bowl and pour the tomato vinaigrette over the top. Toss well, then add the toasted bread and herbs.

Check the seasoning, to taste.

BRAISED FRESH BORLOTTI BEANS

500 g (1 lb 2 oz) fresh borlotti (cranberry) beans, podded weight

50 ml (1¾ fl oz) extra-virgin olive oil, plus extra for drizzling

2 bay leaves

5 garlic cloves, unpeeled and bruised

2 Sun-dried tomatoes (see page 36)

1 rosemary sprig

1 teaspoon salt flakes

There aren't many days of the year when you get to eat this. The minute you see those beautifully pink spotted shells on the shelf, make this. I know it doesn't sound like much, but trust me on this one. The nonnas can't be wrong, either.

Add all the ingredients, except the salt, to a heavy-based saucepan.

Add enough cold water to completely cover the beans, then bring to the boil. Reduce the heat to low and simmer gently for 45–60 minutes, or until tender. If the water begins to dry out before the beans are cooked, just top it up.

Once the beans are tender, add the salt and continue to simmer until the liquid has reduced and slightly thickened.

Remove the bay leaves and rosemary sprig and pop out the garlic cloves from their skins.

Stir, then season well and serve with a big drizzle of extra-virgin olive oil.

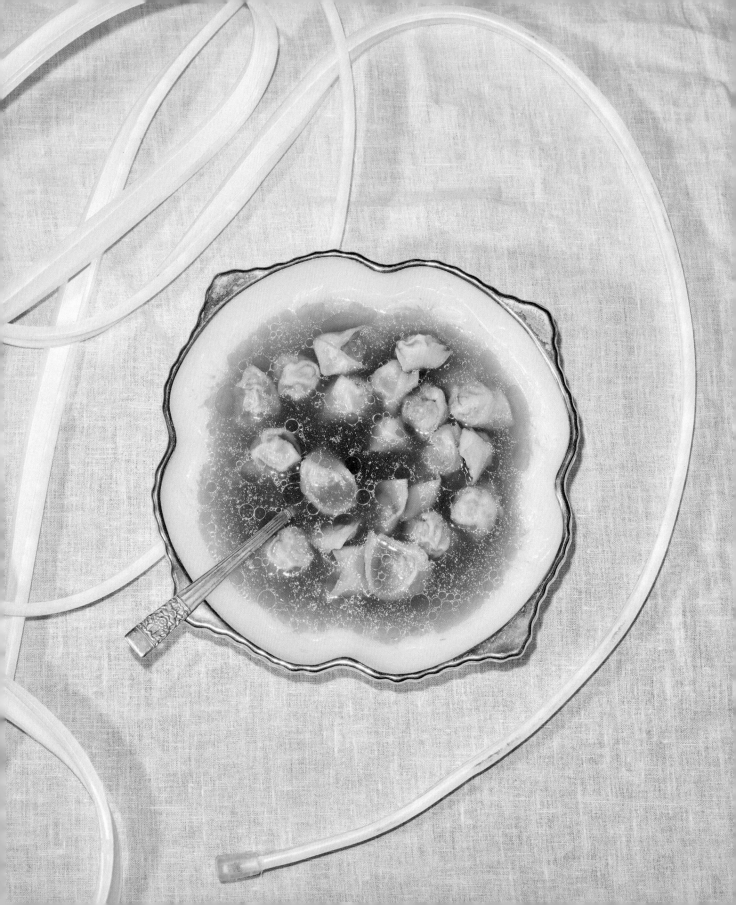

I know it sounds boring, but I am an absolute slut for soup. When I have spent all day on my feet cooking hundreds of meals in a commercial kitchen, the last thing I want to do is make a mess at home (or chew). Soup, in its nutritious, one-pot glory is the answer to that.

Soups get a bad rap because they're usually vegetable purees or chunks floating in broth that are not too dissimilar to baby food. Those are not the soups I like to make.

The soups I eat contain tortellini swimming in a deep, flavoursome brodo; highlight autumn with chestnuts and porcini; use up old bread as in ribollita; or ones that cure me when I'm sick, like pastina. Far from boring.

ZUPPE

SPRING MINESTRONE

60 ml (2 fl oz/¼ cup) extra-virgin olive oil, plus extra for drizzling (optional)

1 brown onion, finely diced

1 leek, white part only, sliced and washed well to remove any dirt

2 celery stalks, diced

1 small fennel bulb, core removed and diced

6 garlic cloves, finely minced

2 litres (68 fl oz/8 cups) vegan chicken or vegetable stock

600 g (1 lb 5 oz) cannellini beans, freshly cooked or tinned and drained

500 g (1 lb 2 oz) mixed chopped green vegetables such as zucchini (courgette), green beans, peas, asparagus and any kind of kale or leafy green that you like

150 g (5½ oz) short pasta such as risoni, tubetti or broken angel hair

¼ bunch of dill, roughly chopped

½ bunch of parsley, roughly chopped

zest and juice of 1 lemon

Gremolata (page 63), to garnish (optional)

This is the rare recipe in the book where I don't instruct you to cook your vegetables into mush. It's light, snappy and delicate. Weird for me, I know.

Heat the oil in a large, heavy-based saucepan over a medium heat then add the onion, leek and a big pinch of salt. Cook for 5 minutes, stirring regularly until they begin to soften.

Next, add the celery and fennel and cook for a further 5 minutes before adding the garlic. Cook out the garlic for an extra minute, then pour in the stock.

Bring the stock up to the boil, then reduce to a gentle simmer and add the cannellini beans and the leafy greens. Cook for 10 minutes, then drop in the remaining veg' and pasta and cook until the vegetables are just tender and the pasta is cooked through. The idea is to keep everything bright and fresh, so don't overdo it.

Season well, then turn off the heat and stir through the chopped herbs and lemon juice.

Garnish with gremolata, if using, or a big drizzle of olive oil.

PASTINA

1.2 litres (41 fl oz) vegan chicken stock or Brodo (page 104)

200 g (7 oz) pastina (tiny star-shaped pasta)

125 ml (4 fl oz/½ cup) soy milk (optional)

50 g (1¾ oz) vegan butter

50 g (1¾ oz/½ cup) grated vegan parmesan, plus extra to serve

drizzle of extra-virgin olive oil

fresh lemon juice

Most people have heard of Jewish penicillin, but the Italians also have a cure. Pastina is much easier to eat while horizontal than the Jewish variety.

Pour the stock into a large saucepan and bring to the boil over a high heat.

Once boiling, pour in the pastina and stir well. Turn down the heat to medium and simmer, stirring the pasta continuously, until the stock is barely covering the pasta and the pasta is cooked through. Add the soy milk (if using), with the butter and parmesan, then beat through till combined. It should look more like a risotto than a soup.

Take off the heat, then season to taste with plenty of salt and pepper. Serve in bowls drizzled with olive oil, a squeeze of lemon juice and extra parmesan.

CHESTNUT & PORCINI SOUP

She might not be the prettiest,
but she's the tastiest.
If you keep this in the fridge,
you are definitely going
to have to thin it out when
you reheat it.

ZUPPE

SERVES 4

25 g (1 oz) dried porcini mushrooms
 soaked in 300 ml (10 fl oz)
 boiling water

60 ml (2 fl oz/¼ cup) extra-virgin
 olive oil, plus extra for drizzling

40 g (1½ oz) vegan butter

4 large shallots, peeled and finely diced

1 carrot, diced

1 celery stalk, diced

200 g (7 oz) button or Swiss brown
 mushrooms, sliced

3 garlic cloves, minced

1 rosemary sprig, leaves chopped

60 ml (2 fl oz/¼ cup) vermouth, sherry
 or marsala

500 g (1 lb 2 oz) fresh chestnuts,
 cooked and peeled

500 g (1 lb 2 oz) potato, peeled and
 diced

1 litre (34 fl oz/4 cups) vegan chicken
 stock

250 ml (8½ fl oz/1 cup) porcini soaking
 liquid

1 bay leaf

In a small bowl, pour the boiling water over the dried porcini and allow to rehydrate for 30 minutes.

While the mushrooms are soaking, heat the oil and butter in a large, heavy-based stockpot over a medium heat.

Add the shallot and cook for 2 minutes before adding the carrot, celery and sliced mushrooms. Season well, then cook for 5 minutes, or until the mushrooms begin to turn a light golden brown.

Add the garlic, rosemary, rehydrated porcini (reserving the liquid), and cook for another minute before deglazing the pot with the vermouth.

Add the chestnuts and potatoes and stir well to coat. Pour in the stock and porcini soaking liquid. (It's best to pass the soaking liquid through a fine-mesh sieve first to collect any grit that may have released from the mushrooms.)

Drop in the bay leaf and bring to the boil.

Reduce to a low simmer and cook until the potatoes and chestnuts are very tender, between 20–30 minutes.

Remove the bay leaf and blend the soup with a handheld blender until very smooth. Add more stock if you prefer a slightly thinner soup. Season well and serve with a drizzle of olive oil.

RIBOLLITA

80 ml (2½ fl oz/⅓ cup) extra-virgin olive oil, plus extra for drizzling

1 brown onion, finely diced

1 carrot, finely diced

½ fennel bulb (approx. 150 g/5½ oz), cored and finely diced

5 garlic cloves, minced

1 teaspoon smoked paprika

1 large tomato, finely diced or tinned (approx. 150 g/5½ oz)

1 bunch of Tuscan kale (cavolo nero), leaves stripped and roughly chopped

80 ml (2½ fl oz/⅓ cup) white wine

1.5 litres (51 fl oz/6 cups) vegan chicken stock

1 rosemary sprig

1 bay leaf

500 g (1 lb 2 oz) cannellini beans, freshly cooked or tinned and drained

250 g (9 oz) stale bread, torn into bite-sized pieces

grated vegan parmesan, to garnish

handful of fresh parsley, finely chopped

You might have noticed at this point that I love soggy food. Soggy bread is no exception. This is soup made from bread, eaten with bread. Extreme? Yeah, I am.

Heat the oil in a large, ovenproof heavy-based saucepan over a medium–low heat and add the onion with a big pinch of salt. Cook for 5 minutes, or until translucent.

Add the carrot, fennel and garlic then season well. Cook for a further 5 minutes, or until the vegetables are tender.

Add the smoked paprika, tomato and kale and stir well to combine. Cook for 2 minutes, or until the leaves begin to soften, then pour in the wine. Cook for another 3 minutes, or until the wine is almost completely reduced.

Pour the stock in then drop in the rosemary, bay leaf and beans. Stir, then bring to the boil. Reduce the heat to low and simmer for 10 minutes.

Preheat the oven to 200°C (390°F).

Add half of the bread and stir through. Simmer for 5 minutes to allow the bread to break down and thicken the soup.

Season the soup to taste, then top the surface of the pan with the remaining bread. Drizzle with olive oil and salt flakes and place in the oven. Bake for 10 minutes, or until the bread is golden.

Remove from the oven and serve topped with parmesan and chopped parsley.

BRODO

220 g (8 oz) celery

350 g (12½ oz) eggplant (aubergine; approx. 1 eggplant), cut into large dice

100 g (3½ oz) carrot, peeled

30 g (1 oz) dried shiitake

120 g (4½ oz) brown onion

1 red onion

150 g (5½ oz) fennel

120 g (4½ oz) broccoli stalks

1 small head garlic, peeled

50 ml (1¾ fl oz) extra-virgin olive oil

20 g (¾ oz) tomato paste (concentrated puree)

1 teaspoon salt flakes

1 teaspoon mushroom seasoning (optional)

This is an intense vegetable stock. Use it in place of meat broths.

Preheat the oven to 160°C (320°F).

Using a food processor or a mandolin, slice all the vegetables very thinly, about 2 mm (⅛ in) thick. Add the veg' to a large roasting tin, then add the oil and tomato paste. Mix well with your hands to evenly coat the veg'. Don't worry about breaking them up.

Roast for 1 hour, stirring every 15 minutes. You want the veg' to get very dark.

Once the veg' is cooked, scrape it into a large saucepan or pot and cover with one litre (34 fl oz/4 cups) of water. Add an extra 250 ml (8½ fl oz/1 cup) water to the roasting tin and scrape off any remaining veg' that may be stuck to the bottom. Pour into the pot.

Bring to the boil, then simmer over a low heat for 30 minutes.

Strain out the solids then pour back into your pot. Season well and add the mushroom seasoning, if using.

PASTA E FAGIOLI

80 ml (2½ fl oz/⅓ cup) extra-virgin olive oil, plus extra for drizzling

1 large brown onion, diced

2 celery stalks, diced

1 carrot, diced

4 garlic cloves, minced

2 tablespoons tomato paste (concentrated puree)

125 ml (4 fl oz/½ cup) white wine

1.5 litres (51 fl oz/6 cups) vegan chicken or vegetable stock

360 g (12½ oz) cooked borlotti (cranberry) beans, half mashed with a fork, half left whole

½ teaspoon dry oregano

1 tablespoon red-wine vinegar

2 bay leaves

1 rosemary sprig

2 thyme sprigs

100 g (3½ oz) tubetti or small shell pasta

¼ bunch of parsley, roughly chopped

⅓ bunch of basil, leaves picked

grated vegan parmesan, to serve (optional)

Who doesn't love a double carb? To me, this is the king. It's a meal on its own, and it's one to give people who claim that soup isn't dinner.

Heat the olive oil in a large, heavy-based saucepan over a medium heat and cook the onion, celery and carrot with a big pinch of salt until soft, about 4 minutes.

Add the garlic and cook out for a minute before adding the tomato paste. Cook for a further 1 minute to caramelise the paste, then pour in the wine and deglaze the pot.

Add the stock and bring to the boil. Reduce the heat to medium and simmer, then stir through the mashed borlotti.

Add the whole borlotti, oregano, vinegar, bay leaves, rosemary and thyme and simmer for 30 minutes, stirring every 5 minutes.

Add the pasta and simmer until cooked. Take off the heat and stir through the basil and parsley.

Season well and serve drizzled with extra-virgin olive oil and some grated parmesan, if using.

Some of the best bites of Italian food come with bread. Think that part at the end of a meal when you break off some bread – what Italians refer to as la scarpetta – to mop up your plate.

What's even better is making the bread yourself. There is no greater pleasure than tearing into a fresh loaf still steaming from the oven, and I want everyone to be able to experience that. The breads and doughs in this chapter are yeast-risen and are very approachable to make and eat. I guarantee you that these recipes are simple enough for you to want to make again and again, and you'll be mixing, baking and eating them all on the same day.

I do, however, include a long-ferment pizza dough recipe for when you want to push the boat out, but that's it. Give it a go. What's that saying, again? Give a man a bread and he will eat for a day. Teach a man to bread and he'll eat for a lifetime?

PANE

SAME-DAY FOCACCIA

This is one of my most replicated recipes from social media. You can have creative freedom with the toppings. Make it as simple or intricate as you like.

Focaccia

9 g (¼ oz) dry yeast (approx. 2½ teaspoons)

15 g (½ oz) agave or sugar

625 ml (21 fl oz/2½ cups) tepid water

160 g (5½ oz) wholemeal (whole-wheat) flour

500 g (1 lb 2 oz/3⅓ cup) 00 flour, or plain (all-purpose) flour

20 g (¾ oz) salt

60 ml (2 fl oz/¼ cup) extra-virgin olive oil, plus extra for greasing and drizzling

My favourite topping

2 garlic cloves, peeled

250 g (9 oz) cherry tomatoes

1 tablespoon capers, drained and rinsed

handful of basil leaves

handful of oregano leaves

1 teaspoon salt flakes

For the focaccia, whisk together the yeast, agave and water, then set aside to bloom for 10 minutes. You want the mixture to become frothy. If it doesn't, your yeast is dead. Go buy more and start again!

Add both flours and the salt to the bowl and mix everything together with a wooden spoon or spatula until you have a rough dough.

Add the oil to another large bowl and drop in the dough. Turn it so it's coated in the oil, then pull up from one side and bring it over to the centre. Turn the bowl and pull again. Do this four times, then flip the dough and cover with a tea (dish) towel.

Leave to prove in a warm place for at least 2 hours, or until the dough has almost doubled in size. Once proved, knock the dough back by punching the air out then repeat the folding process.

Heavily coat a high-sided baking tray with oil, then drop the dough in.

Gently stretch the dough to roughly fit the shape of the tray, then cover. Leave to prove in a warm place for 1 hour.

While the dough is proving, prepare your topping. If using my favourite topping (see ingredients), add all ingredients to a mortar and pestle and grind into a chunky pulp. This can also be done in a food processor or even by just chopping with a knife.

Once the dough has risen in the tray, pour the topping over the dough and press it all over with your fingertips. Cover and prove for a final 30 minutes.

While the dough is proving, preheat the oven to 220°C (430°F).

The dough is ready to bake when you can see large bubbles forming on the surface.

Sprinkle with the salt flakes and bake for about 45 minutes, or until golden brown and crispy on top.

Remove from the oven and drizzle with more olive oil.

Allow to cool in the tray for 20 minutes before removing, then leave to cool to room temperature before cutting.

GLUTEN-FREE FOCACCIA

Why should the coeliacs miss out? That being said, I would only like you to make this if you can find the Caputo brand of gluten-free flour. If you stray from this, you are gonna have a baaaaad time. I promise I am not sponsored by them.

550 g (1 lb 3 oz) Caputo gluten-free flour

2 teaspoons fine salt

300 ml (10 fl oz) soy milk

1 teaspoon white-wine vinegar

300 ml (10 fl oz) tepid water

80 ml (2½ fl oz/⅓ cup) extra-virgin olive oil, plus extra for greasing

1 tablespoon dry yeast

salt flakes, for sprinkling

Combine the flour and salt in the bowl of a stand mixer fitted with the paddle attachment.

In a jug, stir together the soy milk and vinegar and allow to thicken.

In another jug or bowl, whisk the warm water, olive oil and yeast until combined.

Add both wet mixes to the flour and mix until well combined.

Grease a large bowl well with olive oil and dump in the dough. Drizzle with a little more oil and cover with a tea (dish) towel. Leave to prove for about 2 hours, or until doubled in size.

Coat a high-sided baking tray very well with olive oil and turn out the dough. Push it into all corners of the tray and cover again. Prove for another hour.

Cover with whatever flavours you like, and use your fingers to dimple the surface of the dough. Allow to sit for another 10 minutes.

Bake at 200°C (390°F) for 35 minutes, or until golden. Drizzle with some more oil and sprinkle with some salt flakes, then allow to cool for a few minutes before putting on a cooling rack.

Biga

300 g (10½ oz/2 cups) 00 flour

300 g (10½ oz) water

1 g (⅟₁₆ oz) dry yeast
(just under ½ teaspoon)

Dough

300 g (10½ oz) water

15 g (½ oz) salt

400 g (14 oz/2⅔ cups) 00 flour

100 g (3½ oz/⅔ cup) wholemeal
(whole-wheat) flour, or an extra
100 g (3½ oz/⅔ cup) 00 flour

PIZZA DOUGH (LONG FERMENT)

I want to encourage people to stop buying crappy pizza bases for a weeknight dinner. This might be a long-ferment dough, but it doesn't require any more skills than a quick bread does. You can bake off these bases with sugo and freeze them for the future. Just top and heat.

To make the biga, mix the flour, water and yeast in a bowl until well combined, then cover and rest overnight (between 12–24 hours).

For the dough, add the biga, water and salt in a bowl and mix until well combined. Alternatively, add into the bowl of a stand mixer fitted with the dough hook attachment and mix on a low speed until well combined. Add the flour and knead until the dough forms a smooth surface or mix on a low speed for about 5 minutes until it has come together and is relatively smooth, we're not looking for a fully developed dough at this stage. The dough will be quite sticky as this is a high-hydration dough, but it will begin to firm up during fermentation.

Once the dough is roughly kneaded, place in a large oiled container and cover.

Refrigerate for 24 hours.

After 24 hours, remove the dough and cut it into as many pieces as you like.

Place the balls on a well-oiled baking tray and cover. Refrigerate for another 24 hours, or up to 48 hours. (To be honest, I've forgotten I had this in the fridge and used it after 4 days and it was still good.)

When ready to make pizza, remove the dough from the fridge about 1 hour before you're ready to start shaping the pizzas to allow it to come to room temperature.

Shape, top and bake at 220°C (430°F).

To make future you happy as hell, top with Passata (page 16), bake, then freeze. You're welcome.

600 g (1 lb 5 oz) tepid water

7 g (¼ oz) dry yeast

6 g (⅛ oz) sugar

20 g (¾ oz) extra-virgin olive oil,
plus extra for greasing

700 g (1 lb 9 oz/4⅔ cups) plain
(all-purpose) flour, plus extra
for dusting

300 g (10½ oz) fine semolina (not
instant), plus extra for dusting

FAST PIZZA DOUGH

This pizza dough recipe is for the lazy, forgetful, impulsive and disorganised. So, basically all of us. While other recipes have you waiting days, with this recipe you'll be eating in a few hours once you combine your ingredients.

In the bowl of a stand mixer or a large mixing bowl, mix together the water, yeast, sugar and oil.

Add the flour and semolina and slowly mix to combine.

If using a stand mixer, fit the dough hook attachment and knead on a medium speed for about 8 minutes, or until smooth and elastic. If kneading by hand, dump the dough onto a floured surface and knead for at least 10 minutes.

Place the dough in an oiled bowl and cover with a tea (dish) towel. Leave to prove in a warm place for 1–2 hours, or until almost doubled in size.

Knock back the dough by punching or pressing down on it then dump onto a floured surface.

Cut into four to six pieces depending on the size you like your pizzas, then roll into balls.

Either leave them on the bench or transfer to an oiled tray and cover with a tea towel.

Allow the dough balls to prove for another 30 minutes to 1 hour in a warm place.

When the dough is ready, preheat the oven to 220°C (430°F). If you have pizza stones, allow them to heat in the oven.

Dust your work surface with semolina, then working with one ball at a time, press down with your fingers to create a flat disc. Continue stretching the dough, either with the heel of your hand or with a rolling pin.

Once you have your pizza base shaped, place on your preheated pizza stone or a baking tray and top with whatever you like.

Bake until you have pizza.

CIABATTA

Outside of focaccia, this is one of the most recognisable Italian breads in the world. You can either bake this recipe off in one large loaf, or as individual rolls.

extra-virgin olive oil, for greasing

semolina or polenta, for dusting
(if using a pizza stone)

Biga

50 g (1¾ oz/⅓ cup) plain (all-purpose)
flour, plus extra for dusting

2 g (¹⁄₁₆ oz) dry yeast (about
½ teaspoon)

60 g (2 oz) room-temperature water

Dough

400 g (14 oz) tepid water

14 g (½ oz) salt

500 g (1 lb 2 oz/3⅓ cup) 00 flour

To make the biga, mix all the ingredients in a small bowl or jar until well combined. Cover with a cloth and stand for between 4–6 hours.

Once the biga is ready, scoop out into a large mixing bowl and whisk in the water and salt for the dough. Add the flour and stir to combine. At this stage, the dough will be very sticky, but don't be tempted to add more flour. Cover with a tea (dish) towel and rest for 30 minutes in a warm place.

After the first 30 minutes, uncover and begin to fold. Using wet hands, lift one side of the dough and fold into the centre of the ball. Turn the bowl and repeat three more time until all sides of the dough have been folded.

Cover and rest for another 30 minutes. Repeat the folding process another two times, resting for 30 minutes between folds. After the final fold, allow to prove until doubled in size. This will take between 1–2 hours depending on the heat of your room, so just keep an eye on it.

Once doubled in size, knock back with a wet hand by punching or pressing down on it and place the dough into an oiled container about double the size of the dough. Cover with the lid. Refrigerate overnight or for at least 8 hours. The dough can actually be made to this point and kept in the fridge for up to 3 days.

Once ready to bake, remove the dough from the fridge and flour your work surface. Dump the dough out and roughly shape it into a large rectangle. If you're making rolls, cut the rectangle into smaller rectangular pieces once lengthways, then crossways into as many balls as you'd like: three times, eight rolls, etc.

Once you have your dough shaped, generously sprinkle with flour and cover with a tea towel. Allow to prove on the bench for 1½–2½ hours, or until very soft and you can see air bubbles form under the surface of the dough.

When your dough is almost ready, preheat the oven to 200°C (390°F).

Gently flip the dough over, making sure not to remove too much air, then dust the top of the dough with more flour. Place on a baking tray lined with baking paper. If you have a pizza stone, preheat it, dust with semolina or polenta, then place the dough on top. Bake for 15–30 minutes depending on the size of your rolls/loaf.

When it's ready it should be a dark golden colour and the bread should sound hollow when tapped on the bottom.

Allow to cool for 30 minutes before cutting – this is important!

PIADINA

500 g (1 lb 2 oz/3⅓ cups) plain
  (all-purpose) flour

¼ teaspoon bicarbonate of soda
  (baking soda)

10 g (¼ oz) salt

250 ml (8½ fl oz/1 cup) warm water

80 g (2¾ oz) vegetable shortening,
  softened, or use extra-virgin olive oil

The Italian answer to a wrap – except you'll never be disappointed with a piadina.

To a stand mixer add the flour, bicarbonate of soda and salt, and stir to combine, then pour in the water and add the softened shortening.

Using a dough hook, knead the dough for 5–7 minutes, or until smooth and elastic. Cover the bowl with a tea (dish) towel and rest for 30 minutes to 1 hour.

Cut the dough into eight to ten pieces, then roll into balls and roll out to approximately 20 cm (8 in) circles.

Heat a dry frying pan over a medium–high heat and cook for about 2 minutes on the one side and 1 minute on the other side until spotted golden brown.

Eating these fresh is best but if you want to store them, keep in an airtight container or a ziplock bag in the fridge for up to 1 week. Reheat to refresh before eating.

PASTA DURA

Biga

185 g (6½ oz) cold water

4 g (⅛ oz) dry yeast

3 g (⅛ oz) sugar

pinch of salt

380 g (13½ oz/1¼ cups) plain (all-purpose) flour, plus extra for dusting

Dough

190 g (6½ oz) cold water

3 g (⅛ oz) sugar

8 g (¼ oz) salt

30 g (1 oz) extra-virgin olive oil, plus extra for brushing

270 g (9½ oz) fine semolina (not instant), plus extra for dusting

sesame seeds (optional)

This is what bread was for me: the artisanal bread of the eighties. I didn't grow up with sourdough. My options were damper, cheese and vegemite rolls and *this*. And I still know which one I'd rather be eating.

To make the biga, whisk the water, yeast, sugar and salt in a bowl. Mix in the flour, cover, and leave on the bench overnight to ferment. This can also be done first thing in the morning if you'd like to make the bread on the same day. It just needs a minimum of 12 hours.

To make the dough, mix the water, sugar, salt and oil in either the bowl of a stand mixer or a large mixing bowl.

If using a stand mixer, attach the dough hook and slowly incorporate the semolina on a low speed. If mixing by hand, add the semolina and mix in with your hand until fully incorporated.

Once all the semolina is mixed through, tear the biga into small pieces and add to the dough, mixing until it's all incorporated.

Increase the speed of the stand mixer to medium and knead the dough until smooth, about 8 minutes. If mixing by hand, dump the dough on a lightly floured surface and knead until smooth and elastic, about 10 minutes.

Place the dough in a large oiled bowl and cover with a tea (dish) towel. Allow to prove in a warm place till doubled in size, about 1–2 hours.

Knock back the dough by punching it (go full Rocky on it!) then dump onto a floured surface. Shape as desired and place on a baking tray dusted with semolina. For a more traditional style, roughly shape the dough into a large oval then bring up the sides, pinching to join. Flip over and place on the tray, seam side down. Cover and allow to rise for 30–40 minutes before making several cuts across the top of the loaf.

While the final loaf is rising, preheat the oven to 180°C (360°F).

Brush some olive oil over the loaf and sprinkle with sesame seeds, if using, then bake for about 35 minutes, or until golden brown and sounding slightly hollow when tapped on the bottom.

Cool to room temperature before cutting.

FARINATA

350 g (12½ oz) water, at room
temperature

5 g (⅛ oz) salt

freshly cracked black pepper, to taste

300 g (10½ oz/2¾ cups) besan
(chickpea flour)

50 g (1¾ oz) extra-virgin olive oil,
plus extra for coating the pan

1 rosemary sprig, leaves stripped

I wasn't sure if I should include this in the bread section. While it is a flatbread, I also use it as a filling for sandwiches. You can make this batter and cook it immediately, but fermenting it just makes it so much better. There is no more work involved, just time.

Pour the water into a bowl and add the salt and pepper. Slowly stream in the besan, whisking as you pour to avoid any lumps.

Allow to sit in a warm place for at least 2 hours, but preferably overnight, to allow the mixture to slightly ferment. This improves the flavour and is how I prefer it.

When ready to cook, preheat the oven to 220°C (430°F).

Using a ladle, gently remove the foam that has formed on the top of the chickpea batter, then whisk in the olive oil.

Coat a large round baking dish or ovenproof frying pan well with olive oil and heat in the oven until very hot.

Pull the oven rack, leaving the pan in the oven, and quickly pour the batter in. Scatter with rosemary and gently push the shelf back in the oven.

Bake for 10–12 minutes, or until the top is golden brown and crispy but the middle is still slightly soft.

What's an Italian cookbook without pasta? Admittedly, I am not a fresh pasta person. I prefer the bite, texture and convenience of dried pasta, and there are many exceptional ones you can buy off the shelf these days.

But, this isn't just a collection of seasonal sauces. I've also included my recipe for Cacio e pepe (page 126), because I know there'd be a price on my head if I didn't. I had it on the menu at the beginning of the cacio e pepe craze in Australia six years ago, and I haven't been able to take it off since. It's even made its way to Sydney, and something tells me I won't be able to take it off that menu, either.

For those of you who want to try your hand at making pasta, the pizzoccheri dough on page 142 is made with buckwheat and requires no fancy equipment. The dish itself is from Valtellina and is bound together by cabbage and potatoes, exemplifying the regionality of Italy and Switzerland's influence on the plate.

Gnudi is more a method than it is a recipe, but it is well worth the work. I also think it gives gnocchi a run for its money, and it's a lot less temperamental to make.

PASTA

SPAGHETTI POMODORO

140 ml (4½ fl oz) extra-virgin olive oil, plus extra for drizzling

1 brown onion, finely diced

4 garlic cloves, finely sliced

½ teaspoon chilli flakes, or to taste

800 g (1 lb 12 oz) Passata (page 16)

500 g (1 lb 2 oz) dry spaghetti

2 basil sprigs, leaves picked

grated vegan parmesan, to garnish

You might think this is too simple to put in a book, but there is a right way to do things and a wrong way to do things. Guess which way this is.

Heat the olive oil in a large high-sided frying pan over a medium heat. Add the onion, along with a big pinch of salt, and cook until the onion is translucent and just beginning to turn a light golden colour.

Add the garlic and chilli flakes and cook for another minute, then pour in the passata. Reduce the heat to low and simmer, stirring regularly, for 20 minutes, or until the sauce is very thick. You want to cook off most of the moisture, leaving you with a thick, slightly dry paste. Season well.

Cook the pasta in a large saucepan of boiling salted water for 1 minute less than the packet instructions suggest. Remove the pasta directly from the pot of water and drop it into the sauce. Toss very well to coat. If the pasta is a little too dry, add a splash of pasta cooking water.

Throw in the basil leaves and toss again to combine.

Serve garnished with a drizzle of extra-virgin olive oil and grated parmesan.

CACIO E PEPE

500 g (1 lb 2 oz) bucatini or spaghetti

100 g (3½ oz) vegan butter

50 ml (1¾ fl oz) extra-virgin olive oil

4 black garlic cloves, crushed into a paste

2–3 teaspoons freshly cracked black pepper

125 g (4½ oz) silken tofu, blended

150 g (5½ oz) grated vegan parmesan

250 ml (8½ fl oz/1 cup) pasta water

salt flakes, to taste

The chokehold cacio e pepe has had over the last few years means you can find it in any form of food. It's not to say that I don't love cacio e pepe, but I don't believe it's the pinnacle of pasta dishes. And yet, all the while, vegans have missed out – unless you've been to my restaurant, that is. For those who don't live in Australia, this one is for you.

Bring a large saucepan of heavily salted water to the boil. Once boiling, cook the pasta for 1 minute less than what the packet instructions suggest.

A few minutes before the pasta is cooked, place a large frying pan over a medium heat and add the butter and oil. Add the black garlic paste and pepper and cook for 1 minute.

Once cooked, pull the pasta directly from the pot into the frying pan and toss to coat.

Add the blended tofu, parmesan and pasta water. Quickly toss and stir to emulsify the sauce.

Finish with salt flakes, to taste.

BOLOGNESE

125 ml (4 fl oz/½ cup) extra-virgin
olive oil

1 large brown onion, diced

2 celery stalks, finely diced

½ fennel bulb, diced

1 large carrot, diced

20 g (¾ oz/½ cup) dried porcini
mushrooms, soaked and
roughly chopped (reserve the
soaking liquid)

4 large garlic cloves, minced

1 tablespoon chilli flakes, plus an extra
pinch

125 g (4½ oz/½ cup) tomato paste
(concentrated puree)

1 tablespoon sweet paprika

1 tablespoon dried oregano

800 g (1 lb 12 oz) ground vegan mince,
soaked in hot vegan beef stock,
to cover

250 ml (8½ fl oz/1 cup) soy milk

500 ml (17 fl oz/2 cups) red wine

3 × 400 g (14 oz) tins diced tomatoes

700 g (1 lb 9 oz) Passata (page 16)

2 bay leaves

2 teaspoons vegan beef stock powder

2 tablespoons soy sauce

2 tablespoons balsamic

1 tablespoon sugar

2 tablespoons chopped capers

2 tablespoons caper juice (optional)

½ bunch of chopped parsley

½ bunch of torn basil

I wasn't going to put this in, but I am not narcissistic enough
to assume that you own any of my other books. This recipe
has received a few tweaks from the original over the years,
but largely remains unchanged.

Heat the oil in a large, heavy-based pot over a medium heat and cook
off all the veg', along with a big pinch of salt and chilli flakes for about
5 minutes, or until very soft.

Add the tomato paste, paprika and oregano and cook out for a minute.

Add the vegan mince and stir well to coat.

Add the soy milk and deglaze the pan. Once reduced by half, add the
red wine and 250 ml (8½ fl oz/1 cup) of the reserved porcini soaking
liquid and reduce again by half.

Add the remaining ingredients, except for the fresh herbs and bring to the
boil. Reduce to a simmer and cook for 1-2 hours – the longer the better.
Top up with a splash of water if it becomes too thick.

Stir through the fresh herbs and season to taste.

Make jaffles with leftovers or keep for lasagne.

RAGU

60 ml (2 fl oz/¼ cup) extra-virgin olive oil

2 celery stalks, diced

1 brown onion, diced

1 carrot, diced

½ fennel bulb, diced

4 garlic cloves, minced

2 tablespoons capers, with a splash of juice

1 teaspoon chilli flakes

1 teaspoon fennel seeds

400 g (14 oz) vegan mutton (mushroom meat), roughly chopped

2 tablespoons tomato paste (concentrated puree)

250 ml (8½ fl oz/1 cup) soy milk

250 ml (8½ fl oz/1 cup) red wine

700 g (1 lb 9 oz) Passata (page 16)

1 vegan beef stock cube

1 bay leaf

handful of basil and parsley, roughly chopped

Everybody needs a good ragu recipe in their arsenal and this is a good one to knock up on the weekend.

Heat the oil in a frying pan over a low heat and add the celery, onion, carrot and fennel with a pinch of salt. Cook for about 5 minutes, or until the vegetables are beginning to soften. Add the garlic and cook for another minute.

Add the capers, chilli flakes, fennel seeds and mutton. Stir to combine, then cook for about 3 minutes to slightly brown off the meat.

Stir through the tomato paste then deglaze the pan with the soy milk and simmer until reduced by half. Pour in the wine and again, reduce by half.

Pour in the passata and throw in the stock cube and bay leaf. Season to taste with salt and pepper and cook over a low heat for 1 hour, stirring often. Finish with the herbs.

1 kg (2 lb 3 oz) cherry tomatoes

1 whole head of garlic, cloves separated

5 large marjoram or oregano sprigs

150 ml (5 fl oz) extra-virgin olive oil

ROASTED CHERRY TOMATO SAUCE

Make this in the height of summer. If you can stand putting the oven on, throw it all in a tray and forget about it.

Preheat the oven to 200°C (390°F). To a large baking tray, add the cherry tomatoes, garlic, and marjoram and pour the olive oil on top. Season very well with salt and pepper and stir to coat. Roast for 1 hour, stirring every 15 minutes. Ensure that the tomatoes begin to blacken and blister.

Once the tomatoes are soft and totally collapsed, remove from the oven, pop the garlic cloves out of their skins and mash everything with a fork. Remove the stalks of the herbs.

Serve as a simple sauce with pasta or on toasted bread for a warm bruschetta.

CHAMOMILE, SAFFRON & SQUASH SPAGHETTINI

100 g (3½ oz) vegan butter

5 chamomile tea bags, torn open and emptied (or approx. 15 g/½ oz loose-leaf tea)

500 g (1 lb 2 oz) dry spaghettini

2 tablespoons extra-virgin olive oil

1 garlic clove, finely minced

pinch of saffron threads

1 tablespoon fennel seeds, crushed

4 yellow squashes, sliced 5 mm (¼ in) thick

2 green zucchinis (courgettes), sliced in 5 mm (¼ in) rounds

zest and juice of ½ lemon

small handful of mint leaves

Ricotta (page 23; optional)

This is the best warm-weather pasta dish. When I cook it for the restaurant, I throw heaps of chamomile into the cooking water and it turns the pasta this beautiful yellow colour. This is the most delicate dish in this book and it's a great way to use up all those cheap summer zucchinis.

Melt the butter in a small saucepan over a medium heat.

Add half of the chamomile tea to the melted butter and cook over a low heat for about 1 minute. Remove the pan from the heat and allow the tea to infuse in the butter for about 10 minutes.

Pour the butter through a fine-mesh sieve into a bowl. Discard the tea, reserving the butter.

Bring a large pot of water to the boil. Once boiling, add the remaining chamomile tea, turn off the heat and allow it to infuse for 5 minutes.

Using a small sieve, remove as much of the tea as possible, then heavily salt the water.

Return to the boil, then add the spaghettini and cook according to the packet instructions.

While the pasta is cooking, add the chamomile-infused butter and the olive oil to a large frying pan and warm over medium–high heat. Add the garlic, saffron threads and fennel seeds and cook for 1 minute before adding the squash and zucchini.

Fry, tossing often, until the vegetables are just beginning to soften.

Using a slotted pasta spoon or tongs, remove the cooked pasta directly from the pot and add it to the frying pan. Season well.

Add the lemon juice and zest to the pasta and stir through. Using a ladle, add about 125 ml (4 fl oz/½ cup) of the chamomile pasta water and quickly toss through the pasta to emulsify the sauce.

Add the mint leaves and give the pan a quick toss.

To serve, place the pasta on plates and spoon over any remaining sauce. If using the ricotta, scatter over the pasta just before serving.

BORLOTTI & FREGOLA

80 ml (2½ fl oz/⅓ cup) extra-virgin olive oil, plus extra for drizzling

5 garlic cloves, thickly sliced

2 dried chillies, crushed

2 tomatoes, roughly chopped

400 g (14 oz) freshly cooked or tinned borlotti (cranberry) beans

2 bay leaves

3 thyme sprigs

200 g (7 oz) dry fregola, par-cooked

500 ml (17 fl oz/2 cups) vegan chicken or vegetable stock

¼ bunch of parsley, roughly chopped

Cook the fregola a lot longer than you think you need to. For those unfamiliar with fregola, you might mistake it for cous cous. It's toasted, dry pasta that lends dishes an incredible chewy texture. Borlotti is my preferred bean for this dish, but feel free to use whatever legume you have on hand.

Heat the oil in a large, heavy-based saucepan over a medium heat, then add the garlic and crushed chilli. Cook till the garlic begins to turn a light golden brown, about 1–2 minutes.

Add the chopped tomatoes and season well. Cook until the tomatoes begin to dry out, about 5 minutes.

Add the bortlotti beans, bay leaves, thyme and par-cooked fregola.

Pour the stock in and reduce the heat to low and simmer gently until the liquid has reduced by half.

Stir through the chopped parsley and season well.

Serve topped with plenty of extra-virgin olive oil.

SAUSAGE & BEAN GIGLI

80 ml (2½ fl oz/⅓ cup) extra-virgin
olive oil

250 g (9 oz) vegan sausages,
casings removed

1 brown onion, finely diced

½ fennel bulb, core removed,
finely diced

3 garlic cloves, finely sliced

1 rosemary sprig

½ teaspoon chilli flakes

600 g (1 lb 5 oz) cooked cannellini
beans, freshly cooked or tinned
and drained

150 ml (5 fl oz) white wine

250 ml (8½ fl oz/1 cup) vegan chicken
or vegetable stock

1 bunch of Tuscan kale (cavolo nero),
leaves stripped and torn

500 g (1 lb 2 oz) gigli pasta, or short
tube pasta

50 g (1¾ oz) vegan butter

30 g (1 oz) grated vegan parmesan

You need to have access to vegan sausages to make this dish. They can't be those vegetable ones, either. It has to be mock meat-based or this won't turn out.

Pour half the oil into a shallow dutch oven and place over a medium heat. Add the sausage meat and break up with a wooden spoon. Season well and cook until golden brown, about 3 minutes. Pull the sausage meat out of the pan and set aside.

Add the remaining oil to the pan and cook off the onion and fennel until beginning to soften, then add the garlic, rosemary and chilli flakes and cook for another 2 minutes.

Pour the cannellini beans in and stir to combine.

Pour in the wine and deglaze the pan. Using a wooden spoon, crush about one-third of the beans, then pour in the stock.

Add the cavolo nero, stir to coat, then cover the pan. Simmer over a low heat for 5 minutes.

While the sauce is cooking, cook the pasta according to the packet instructions in a large pot of boiling salted water, stopping 2 minutes before the recommended time. Drain, and return to the pot, then add the parmesan. Toss through, along with a splash of pasta water, and season well.

Add the sausage and butter to the sauce and stir through.

LASAGNE VERDI

800 g–1 kg (1 lb 12 oz–2 lb 3 oz) mixed greens (I like to use silverbeet/Swiss chard, spinach or Tuscan kale)

60 ml (2 fl oz/¼ cup) extra-virgin olive oil

½ brown onion, finely diced

5 garlic cloves, minced

60 g (2 oz/¼ cup) vegan butter

50 g (1¾ oz/⅓ cup) plain (all-purpose) flour

70 ml (2¼ fl oz) white wine

500 ml (17 fl oz/2 cups) vegan milk

500 ml (17 fl oz/2 cups) vegan chicken or vegetable stock

60 g (2 oz) vegan parmesan

1 × quantity Spinach pasta dough (page 140) or any premade lasagne sheets

200 g (7 oz) Ricotta (page 23; optional)

Pesto

1 garlic clove

25 g (1 oz) pine nuts, toasted

1 bunch of basil, leaves picked

150 ml (5 fl oz) extra-virgin olive oil

20 g (¾ oz) vegan parmesan

This is the spring version of a traditional lasagne. It's lighter, fresher and won't send you into a coma. Feel free to use the Fresh pasta dough (page 138), Spinach pasta dough (page 140) or instant lasagne sheets.

Preheat the oven to 180°C (360°F).

Blanch the greens, drain and then shock in a bowl of iced water.

Heat the oil in a large frying pan over a low heat and cook off the onion and garlic till lightly golden, then add the blanched greens. Season with salt and pepper and cook for 2 minutes. Remove from the pan and set aside.

To make a bechamel sauce, in a large heavy-based saucepan, melt the butter over a medium heat. Add the flour and cook for 2 minutes, stirring constantly. Pour in the wine, continuing to stir constantly until the wine has almost completely evaporated. Remove from the heat, then slowly whisk in the milk and the stock, ensuring the consistency is as smooth as possible. Once all the liquid is incorporated, return to the stove over a low heat and gently simmer for 5 minutes, stirring regularly. Set aside.

To make the pesto, add the garlic and a pinch of salt to a mortar and use the pestle to pound into a paste. Add the pine nuts and roughly crush them before slowly adding in handfuls of the basil leaves until they are bruised. Slowly start adding in the olive oil, pounding as you go until you have a cohesive mixture. Add the parmesan and season to taste. Alternatively, you can blitz all the pesto ingredients except the oil in a food processor until a rough paste is formed, then slowly add the olive oil until you have a cohesive mixture.

Roll out the spinach dough into one long sheet 3 mm (⅛ in) thick. Cut to fit your desired baking dish – aim for 1 large sheet per layer. Blanch in salted boiling water for 30 seconds. Remove and lay out on a clean tea (dish) towel and lightly brush each side with olive oil. Repeat with the remaining sheets.

Line a 33 × 22 × 7 cm (13 × 9 × 2.5 in) baking dish with baking paper. Start assembling by laying down the first pasta sheet. Layer with the greens, bechamel sauce, parmesan, and dot with the ricotta, if using. Repeat layers until you have reached the top of the dish. Finish with a layer of bechamel. Cover with baking paper and foil and bake in the oven for 45 minutes to 1 hour. To check that it's done, push a knife through the centre and if it goes through without resistance, it's ready. Remove from the oven and allow to rest for 10 minutes to set properly.

Whatever you don't eat, freeze.

FRESH PASTA DOUGH

150 g (5½ oz) plain (all-purpose) flour, plus extra for dusting

180 g (6½ oz) fine semolina (not instant)

190 g (6½ oz) warm water

5 g (⅛ oz) fine salt

10 g (¼ oz) extra-virgin olive oil

Basic, I know. But it's good to know the basics. You don't need eggs to make good fresh pasta.

Combine all the ingredients in a food processor and pulse until you have a crumbly texture.

Dump the mixture onto a floured surface and knead with your hands until smooth and elastic, about 6–8 minutes.

If the dough is too dry, add a little more water. If it's too wet, add a little extra flour.

Roll your dough into a ball and wrap in plastic wrap, then refrigerate for at least 30 minutes.

When ready to use, cut your dough into two pieces and either roll through a pasta roller to your desired thickness (see page 141) before cutting, or simply roll out with a rolling pin and cut by hand.

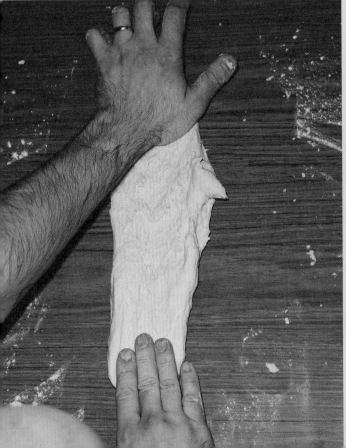

SPINACH PASTA DOUGH

If you have a food processor, this is one of the easiest things to make. Do it. Use that oversized, useless machine taking up space on your kitchen counter.

**MAKES APPROX.
575 G (1 LB 4 OZ)**

250 g (9 oz/1¾ cups) 00 flour, plus
    extra for dusting

1 bunch of spinach, stalks removed
    (approx. 325 g/11½ oz)

pinch of salt

Wash the spinach well in cold water, then dry completely either in a salad spinner or between tea (dish) towels.

Put the flour in a food processor then add the spinach leaves and salt.

Blitz for a few minutes. It will start off quite powdery, then begin to come together, so don't be tempted to add water. It will take a few minutes.

Once it has formed a ball, remove the lid and feel the dough. If it feels soft and holds together, it's ready. If it's a little dry and crumbly, add a little more spinach or a drizzle of water and blitz again.

Dust your bench with the extra flour, or semolina, and tip the dough out and knead for 5–7 minutes. It will feel quite stiff at first, so knead until it becomes smooth and elastic.

Cover in plastic wrap and let it rest for at least 30 minutes. (This can be done up to 1 day in advance.)

Once you're ready to cook, cut the dough into three pieces. Start by feeding one piece through the widest setting of your pasta roller. Make sure to dust the dough well with flour so that it doesn't stick.

Roll it through once, then fold the dough in half on itself and pass it through again. Lower the dial settings, one step at a time, until you get the thickness of your choosing. Pasta rollers will vary, so I'm giving directions for a common-style Mercato Atlas bench roller. If you have something different, just play around and use your best judgement.

For spaghetti, roll to dial three or four; fettuccine, five or six; lasagne sheets, roll to dial three, and for filled pastas like ravioli, roll to dial six or seven depending on the size of your filled pasta. Ultimately, it's up to your personal preference, so have a play. If you find that you've rolled it too thin, just fold the sheet back over itself and pass through on a slightly higher setting.

Once you have achieved your desired thickness, cut the pasta according to the shape you're making. For spaghetti, add the cutting attachment and pass it through. Dust the cut pasta with more flour and place in little bundles on the bench. If you're making lasagne or filled pasta, leave as is and cut to your desired lengths.

To cook, bring a large saucepan of heavily salted water to the boil. Fresh pasta doesn't take long to cook. Depending on the thickness it will be anywhere between 2–5 minutes. Basically, when it floats, it's ready. Be sure not to overcook, as overcooked fresh pasta is rubbish.

PIZZOCCHERI

600 g (1 lb 5 oz) potatoes, peeled and roughly diced into 2 cm (¾ in) cubes

300 g (10½ oz) savoy cabbage, sliced into 1 cm (½ in) strips

150 g (5½ oz) vegan butter

2 tablespoons extra-virgin olive oil

1 brown onion, finely sliced

2 garlic cloves, finely minced

200 g (7 oz) your favourite vegan melting cheese, diced

50 g (1¾ oz) vegan parmesan, grated

Pasta

350 g (12½ oz/3 cups) buckwheat flour, plus extra for dusting

100 g (3½ oz/⅔ cup) 00 flour

large pinch of salt

220 ml (7½ fl oz) warm water (just above a tepid temperature)

On my last trip to Italy, I spent time in the town of Bolzano. A three-hour drive through the Alps will take you to a town called Teglio, right on the Swiss-Italian border. Back in the 1600s, buckwheat was a staple, but by the 1950s it was replaced with more lucrative crops, like wheat. Traditional recipes changed over the years, with only a few places still making pizzoccheri the traditional way with pure buckwheat flour.

To make the pasta, add the buckwheat flour, 00 flour and salt to a bowl. Mix to combine.

Slowly pour in the water and incorporate it into the flour until you have a rough ball of dough.

Turn out onto a floured surface and use a rolling pin to roll the dough out until it's about 3 mm (⅛ in) thick.

Using a sharp knife, trim the edges of the dough and dust the surface with more buckwheat or 00 flour to prevent sticking, then cut into 5 cm (2 in) strips.

Stack the strips on top of each other and cut into 1 cm (½ in) rectangular pieces. Set aside.

Place the potatoes in a large pot of cold salted water and bring to the boil.

After the potatoes have been cooking for 5 minutes, add the cabbage and cook for another 5 minutes.

While the veg' is cooking, heat the butter and olive oil in a large frying pan over a medium heat. Add the onion and cook till it begins to turn a light golden brown, then add the garlic and cook for another 1–2 minutes, then set aside.

Add the pasta to the potatoes and cabbage and cook for a further 3 minutes, or until the pasta floats to the surface.

Using a slotted spoon, pull the pasta and vegetables out of the pot and drop into the frying pan. Add the cheese and parmesan and mix it all together until the cheese has melted and the garlic butter has coated everything. If it looks dry, add a little liquid from the veg' cooking pot to loosen.

Season well with salt and freshly ground black pepper and serve immediately.

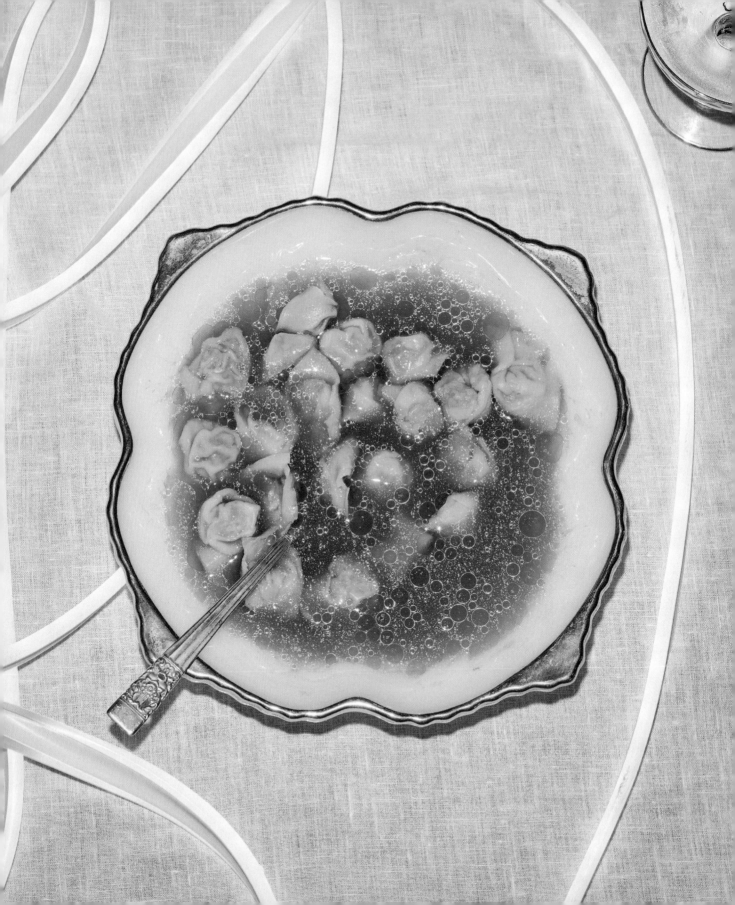

TORTELLINI

125 g (4½ oz) ground vegan meat of your choice

100 g (3½ oz/1 cup) finely grated vegan parmesan

1 large garlic clove, finely grated or minced

½ teaspoon ground fennel

30 g (1 oz) fresh oregano, finely chopped, use 5 g (⅛ oz) dried oregano

pinch of ground nutmeg

pinch of chilli flakes (optional)

1 × quantity Fresh pasta dough (page 138)

plain (all-purpose) flour, dusting

Feel like a little project? This is a good one. While you can fill these with whatever you like, the following recipe is for a classic, vegan meat-filled tortellini that you can serve with your favourite sauce or in soups. Make them as small or large as you like.

Begin by making the tortellini filling. In a bowl, combine the ground meat, parmesan, garlic, fennel, oregano, nutmeg and chilli flakes, if using, then season well with salt and pepper.

Mix well with your hands until everything is well combined into a smooth mixture. Cover with plastic wrap and refrigerate for at least 2 hours to allow the flavours to develop.

Cut the pasta dough into 5 cm (2 in) squares. Place on a lightly floured tray and cover with a cloth to prevent it from drying out.

Spoon 1 teaspoon of the filling into the centre of each pasta square, then dip your finger in water and lightly trace around the edges of the pasta. Fold one corner across to the opposite corner to form a triangle. Press down on the edges firmly to seal and remove any air bubbles.

Next, pull the bottom two corners together to form the tortellini. Place back on your floured tray and repeat with the remaining dough and filling.

To cook the tortellini, bring a large saucepan of heavily salted water to the boil over a high heat. Carefully transfer the tortellini to the water and cook, gently stirring often to prevent sticking, until all of the tortellini begin to float to the surface. This will take about 5 minutes.

Serve in Brodo (page 104) or tossed through your choice of sauce.

GNUDI

500 g (1 lb 2 oz) medium-firm tofu, pressed to remove as much liquid as possible

50 g (1¾ oz/½ cup) grated vegan parmesan

¼ teaspoon baking powder

½ teaspoon black salt

1 teaspoon salt flakes

½ teaspoon ground white pepper

1 teaspoon egg replacer mixed with 2 tablespoons water

50 g (1¾ oz) semolina or gluten-free flour, plus extra for dusting

Gnocchi's hotter sister. There, I said it.

Place everything in a food processor and blitz until well combined and smooth.

Dust a baking tray liberally with extra semolina and, using two spoons, scoop out and roughly shape the mixture into ovals, then place on the tray.

Roll the gnudi in the semolina and gently shape into balls, then flatten slightly. You should have about twenty. Feel free to make them whatever size you like.

Place on a plate or baking tray lined with baking paper and refrigerate for 30 minutes. This will help create a thin skin on the gnudi.

Bring a large saucepan of salted water to a gentle simmer.

Carefully drop the gnudi into the simmering water, being sure not to overcrowd the pan.

Once the gnudi float to the surface, after about 4–5 minutes, they're cooked. Scoop them out with a slotted spoon onto a serving plate.

I recommend serving these with toasted hazelnuts and marjoram fried in browned butter but they're just as delicious served with the Roasted cherry tomato sauce (page 129).

I won't lie to you, I've taken some creative licence in labelling these dishes mains because really, any dish in this book can be a main if you make enough of it. The thing is, this is usually the section of the menu in an Italian restaurant that is definitely not vegan-friendly. So, I've taken an Italian approach to robust vegetables and legumes to turn them into impressive mains that you would feel comfortable to dish up at a dinner party.

A word of warning: these dishes are generous in portion and are designed to serve four to six big eaters. I'd advise halving the recipes if you're just cooking for yourself, or making space in your freezer to stop you from ordering takeout on those nights you have nothing left to give. All the recipes in this chapter are freezer-friendly and can keep for up to three months.

While these dishes are designed to impress, I've definitely cooked them for myself and eaten them out of a bowl on my couch in front of the TV.

SECONDI

WHOLE ROASTED EGGPLANT WITH OLIVE SALAD

2 × 600 g (1 lb 5 oz) eggplants (aubergines), or use 4 × 350 g (12½ oz) ones

375 g (13 oz) mixed pitted olives, roughly chopped

60 g (2 oz) capers, drained and roughly chopped

50 ml (1¾ fl oz) red-wine vinegar

1 teaspoon sugar

60 ml (2 fl oz/¼ cup) chilli oil

2 tablespoons extra-virgin olive oil, plus extra for rubbing

½ bunch of parsley, roughly chopped

¼ bunch of mint, roughly chopped

The olive salad is a nod to the muffuletta – another one of those classic Italian-American dishes. When served over a slowly roasted, whole eggplant (aubergine), you have the most indulgent main for minimal effort. Make this a centrepiece for your next dinner party.

Preheat the oven to 200°C (390°F). Line a baking tray with foil or baking paper.

Poke several holes in the eggplants with a sharp knife or fork. This will stop them from exploding in the oven. Rub with a little olive oil and salt, then place on the baking tray.

Roast in the oven for 40 minutes to 1 hour depending on the size of the eggplants. Turn them every 15 minutes until they are soft and collapsed.

Once cooked, remove from the oven and allow to cool slightly while you make the olive salad.

For the salad, combine all the remaining ingredients in a bowl and season to taste.

To serve, cut just below the stem and just above the base three-quarters of the way through, then make another cut lengthways, also three-quarters of the way through. Open up the eggplant, skin side down, with the soft flesh facing up. Roughly score the flesh with a sharp knife, then season with salt and pepper.

Place the eggplants on a platter or individual plates and spoon over the olive salad.

BRAISED PINE MUSHROOMS

2 tablespoons vegan butter

100 ml (3½ fl oz) extra-virgin olive oil

1 small carrot (about 120 g/4½ oz), finely diced

1 celery stalk, finely diced

1 large brown onion, finely diced

4 garlic cloves, minced

1 tablespoon capers, drained and finely minced

1 tablespoon tomato paste (concentrated puree)

125 ml (4 fl oz/½ cup) white wine

1 litre (34 fl oz/4 cups) vegan chicken or vegetable stock

1 rosemary sprig, leaves finely chopped

2 thyme sprigs

2 bay leaves

800 g (1 lb 12 oz) pine mushrooms, thickly sliced (if pine mushrooms are unavailable, substitute with any firm mushroom and add 1 tablespoon porcini mushroom powder)

¼ bunch of parsley, roughly chopped

When I was writing this book, it was mushroom season and there were pines everywhere. Go foraging, or this recipe could get expensive. Feel free to use any meaty mushrooms that you like, or that grow around you, as long as you know what you're picking. Don't let the 'pine' in the mushrooms deter you from making this.

Heat the butter and olive oil in a shallow dutch oven or large frying pan over a medium–high heat and cook off the carrot, celery and onion, along with a large pinch of salt. Sauté for a few minutes until the veg' begins to soften and the onion begins to turn slightly golden.

Add the garlic and capers and cook out for another minute, then stir through the tomato paste. Continue to sauté until the tomato paste begins to caramelise and go slightly dark.

Pour in the wine and deglaze the pan, then simmer until the wine has reduced by half. Pour in the stock and add the rosemary, thyme and bay leaves. Season well and cover the pan with a lid. Reduce the heat to low and simmer for 20 minutes.

Remove the lid and add the sliced pine mushrooms. Check the level of liquid in the pot. It should only just reach the top of the mushrooms.

Cook for a further 10–15 minutes over a medium–low heat with the lid off, stirring every few minutes. Continue to cook until the liquid has reduced to a thick sauce that coats the mushrooms generously.

Stir through the chopped parsley and check the seasoning.

WILD MUSHROOM RISOTTO

If you're not sick of eating mushroom risotto, this is the benchmark. There is shit mushroom risotto, and then there is this. Make this and you'll never order it in a restaurant again.

Mushrooms

50 g (1¾ oz) vegan butter

50 ml (1¾ fl oz) extra-virgin olive oil

500 g (1 lb 2 oz) mixed mushrooms, preferably wild, left whole or chopped depending on size

2 thyme sprigs, leaves stripped

250 ml (8½ fl oz/1 cup) water

Risotto

1.2 litres (41 fl oz) hot vegan chicken stock

2 tablespoons extra-virgin olive oil, plus extra for drizzling

2 shallots, finely diced

3 garlic cloves, minced

15 g (½ oz) dried porcini, rehydrated in 150 ml (5 fl oz) boiling water for 30 minutes

2 thyme sprigs, leaves stripped

250 g (9 oz) arborio rice

150 ml (5 fl oz) white wine

30 g (1 oz) vegan parmesan, grated

25 g (1 oz) vegan butter

For the mushrooms, heat the butter and oil in a heavy-based saucepan or pot over a high heat.

Add the mushrooms along with the thyme and a large pinch of salt and cracked pepper. Fry until a light golden brown, then pour the water in and bring to the boil.

Simmer until the water has been fully absorbed and the mushrooms begin to fry again. Cook until the mushrooms have developed a light golden-brown colour in places, then remove from the pan and place to the side in a bowl.

Place the chicken stock in a saucepan set over a low heat to keep warm.

In the same pan that you cooked the mushrooms in, heat the oil for the risotto over a medium heat and add the shallot and garlic along with a pinch of salt. Cook for about 2 minutes, or until they have softened.

Squeeze out the porcini mushrooms to remove the excess water, but reserve the bowl of soaking water. Roughly chop the porcini. Add to the pan along with the thyme and stir to combine.

Scatter in the rice and stir to coat in the oil. Fry, stirring continuously, until the outer edges of the rice grains begin to go translucent.

Pour in the wine and cook over a medium–low heat, stirring constantly until completely absorbed, then add the reserved porcini liquid and reduce.

Begin adding the stock, two ladles at a time, stirring often. Once the rice has absorbed the stock, add another two ladles, and so on.

Continue this process until the rice is fully cooked and creamy. You want the risotto to be fairly loose and to smoothly drop off the spoon when lifted from the pot.

Fold in three-quarters of the cooked mixed mushrooms that you set aside.

Add the parmesan and butter, and season to taste with salt and pepper. Stir to mix through, then take off the heat. Cover with a lid or tea (dish) towel and allow to stand for 2 minutes.

To serve, place the risotto on a plate or in a bowl, then top with the remaining cooked mushrooms, a drizzle of olive oil and freshly cracked pepper.

MUSHROOM MARSALA

100 g (3½ oz) vegan butter

250 g (9 oz) cipollini, peeled and quartered

1 kg (2 lb 3 oz) mixed mushrooms, thickly sliced or torn

25 g (1 oz) dried porcini, rehydrated in boiling water for 30 minutes (reserve the soaking liquid)

4 thyme sprigs

4 garlic cloves, finely sliced

60 g (2 oz) plain (all-purpose) flour

500 ml (17 fl oz/2 cups) marsala

250 ml (8½ fl oz/1 cup) vegan beef or vegetable stock

125 ml (4 fl oz/½ cup) vegan cream

chopped parsley, to garnish

When I think about marsala, it makes me think of *The Godfather* and *Goodfellas*. This is definitely an Italian-American Hollywood dish for me, but it is still very authentically Italian, too. It's on the sweeter side of the savoury scale, but that's what makes it so appealing.

Melt the butter in a shallow dutch oven over a medium–high heat, then add the cipollini and the fresh and dry mushrooms. Season well, then cook until the mushrooms are beginning to colour, about 5 minutes.

Add the thyme then pour in just enough water to cover the mushrooms. Simmer until the water has completely evaporated.

Once the liquid has evaporated, continue to cook the mushrooms until they begin to fry again, then add the garlic. Cook out for 1 minute, then scatter the flour on top. Stir to combine, then toast the flour for 1 minute before deglazing with the marsala.

Once the marsala has reduced by half, add the stock. Stir well and reduce the heat to low. Cook for 5 minutes, or until the sauce has thickened, then pour in the cream and stir. Be sure not to bring the sauce back to the boil at this point, or it will split. Simmer over a low heat for another 3 minutes, then add the fresh parsley and season to taste with salt and pepper.

It's great served on fried or soft polenta, or through pasta.

TORTA PASQUALINA

This is a two-for-one recipe. Follow the recipe as is and you have the complete dish. It is perfect for taking on a picnic as it is great served at room temperature. The filling alone is an exceptional side dish. Hint hint: if you can't be bothered making the dough. (This recipe is pictured on page 148.)

Olive oil dough

460 g (1 lb) plain (all-purpose) flour, plus extra for dusting

15 g (½ oz) salt

240 g (8½ oz) cold water

70 g (2½ oz) extra-virgin olive oil, plus extra for brushing

100 g (3½ oz) breadcrumbs

salt flakes, for sprinkling

Filling

1 bunch of silverbeet (Swiss chard), stalks chopped and reserved

1 bunch of rapa

1 bunch of Tuscan kale (cavolo nero)

60 ml (2 fl oz/¼ cup) extra-virgin olive oil

2 brown onions, finely diced

5 garlic cloves, finely sliced

300 g (10½ oz) firm silken tofu

150 ml (5 fl oz) vegan cream

30 g (1 oz) pine nuts, toasted

¼ teaspoon ground nutmeg

50 g (1¾ oz) vegan parmesan, grated

zest and juice of 1 lemon

handful of mint leaves, finely chopped

To make the dough, place the flour and salt in a large mixing bowl and stir to combine.

Create a well in the centre and pour in the water and olive oil. Mix with a wooden spoon or your hands until the dough comes together, then turn it out onto a floured surface and knead for a few minutes until smooth. If it feels too sticky, add a little extra flour.

Wrap the dough in plastic wrap and refrigerate while you make the filling. (This can be done a day or two in advance.)

For the filling, bring a large saucepan of salted water to the boil over a high heat.

Working in batches, blanch the leafy greens for 5 minutes, placing into a colander as you go. No need to refresh in iced water. Continue until all the greens have been blanched.

Heat the oil in a large frying pan or wide, heavy-based pot over a medium–high heat.

Add the onion and chopped silverbeet stalks along with a big pinch of salt and cook for 10 minutes, stirring from time to time, until the onion and stalks are soft and beginning to colour.

Add the garlic and cook for another 2 minutes.

While the garlic is cooking, squeeze out as much water from the blanched greens as possible and roughly chop.

Add the chopped greens to the pan and stir well to combine all the ingredients.

Add the tofu to the greens and, using the back of a wooden spoon, break up into small pieces, then pour in the cream. Stir well to evenly distribute the ingredients, then add the pine nuts, nutmeg and parmesan, and season to taste with salt and pepper.

Cook over a medium–high heat until the cream has reduced by half and clings to the mixture.

Add the lemon juice and zest, then the mint. Season again if needed and place the mixture into a bowl to cool to room temperature.

To build the torta, first preheat the oven to 180°C (360°F).

Cut the dough into four pieces and roll each piece into a thin 30 cm (12 in) circle about 2–3 mm (1/16–1/8 in) thick.

Line a round pizza tray or baking tray with baking paper and place the first circle of pastry down. Brush with olive oil and top with another circle of pastry.

Next, scatter the breadcrumbs on top of the pastry, leaving a 5 cm (2 in) border, then pile the greens over the breadcrumbs and top with another circle of pastry. Brush with more olive oil, then finish with the last circle of pastry. Press the edges to seal and trim any uneven edges.

Crimp or fold the edges, then brush with olive oil and sprinkle with salt flakes.

Using a small, pointed knife, cut a 'v' shape on the centre of the top to let out steam.

Bake for 50 minutes to 1 hour, or until the pastry is dark golden brown.

Allow to cool for at least 20 minutes before slicing. It's great served at room temperature.

TRIPPA ALLA ROMANA

100 ml (3½ fl oz) extra-virgin olive oil, plus extra for drizzling

1 large brown onion, finely diced

1 large carrot, finely diced

2 celery stalks, finely diced

3 large garlic cloves, finely sliced

1 teaspoon fennel seeds

½–1 teaspoon chilli flakes

1 teaspoon smoked paprika

1 teaspoon dried oregano

2 bay leaves

1 tablespoon tomato paste (concentrated puree)

250 ml (8½ fl oz/1 cup) white wine

300 g (10½ oz) Passata (page 16)

250 ml (8½ fl oz/1 cup) vegan chicken stock

2 tablespoons vegan fish sauce

30 g (1 oz) dried cloud mushrooms, rehydrated in boiling water for 30 minutes

10 g (¼ oz) dried white wood-ear fungus (if unavailable replace with another 10 g/¼ oz cloud mushrooms), rehydrated in boiling water for 30 minutes

handful of mint leaves

handful of celery leaves from the inner stems (optional)

grated vegan parmesan, to serve (optional)

There is no tripe in the making of this tripe. It's hard enough to convince meat-eaters to try it, let alone vegans. Trust me, it's all about the texture. Enter, white cloud mushrooms.

Heat the oil in a large shallow dutch oven or deep frying pan over a low heat.

Add the onion, carrot and celery with a pinch of salt and sauté over a medium heat until the onion becomes soft and translucent, about 5 minutes. Add the garlic and cook out for another minute.

Add the fennel seeds, chilli flakes, smoked paprika, dried oregano and bay leaves. Stir well to combine, then add the tomato paste and cook for another minute.

Add the white wine and bring to a simmer. Reduce by half, then add the passata. Simmer for another 5 minutes, then add the stock and fish sauce. Season with salt and pepper and reduce the heat to low, then continue simmering for 15–20 minutes, stirring occasionally.

While the sauce is simmering, drain the mushrooms and trim any tough pieces that may contain dirt. Cut the cloud mushrooms into large, bite-sized pieces. Slice the white wood-ear fungus into thin strips, if using. Add the mushrooms to the sauce and stir to combine.

Simmer the mixture over a low heat until the mushrooms are tender and the sauce has reduced, about 20 minutes. Season with salt and pepper.

Garnish with the mint and celery leaves and drizzle with olive oil. Serve with grated parmesan or tossed through a pasta like cavatelli, if desired.

PICCATA

plain (all-purpose) flour, for dusting

½ lemon, sliced, to garnish

Dry ingredients

150 g (5½ oz) vital wheat gluten

2 teaspoons onion powder

1 teaspoon garlic powder

½ teaspoon ground white pepper

1 teaspoon mushroom seasoning
(you can find this at most
Asian grocery stores)

Wet ingredients

140 g (5 oz) medium-firm tofu, pressed

160 ml (5½ fl oz) water

30 g (1 oz) white miso paste

25 ml (¾ fl oz) vegetable oil

5 g (⅛ oz) salt

1½ teaspoons vegan chicken stock
powder

10 g (¼ oz) caster (superfine) sugar

Poaching liquid

2 litres (68 fl oz/8 cups) water

3 teaspoons vegan chicken stock
powder

1 rosemary sprig

2 thyme sprigs

1 bay leaf

1 tablespoon soy sauce

Piccata sauce

50 g (1¾ oz) vegan butter

2 shallots, finely diced

2 garlic cloves, finely minced

60 g (2 oz) plain (all-purpose) flour

600 ml (20½ fl oz) vegan chicken stock

100 ml (3½ fl oz) lemon juice

70 g (2½ oz) small capers in brine,
drained

¼ bunch of parsley, finely chopped

Note

These fillets can be crumbed and used
for schnitzels, if you like.

Here's another vegan meat recipe. It's a simple one to make at home and double if you want some in the freezer for a rainy day. If you crumb and fry the chicken and drench it with the marsala from page 154, you will have a very good time. (If you don't know how to crumb chicken, go look at the fried olive recipe on page 47.)

Combine all the dry ingredients in a large mixing bowl.

Add all of the wet ingredients to a blender and blitz until very smooth.

Pour the tofu liquid into the dry ingredients, bring together into a dough and knead for 5 minutes.

Cover and allow to rest for 30 minutes before shaping. (This can be done up to 1 day in advance and rested in the fridge overnight.)

Cut into four to eight pieces, depending on how large you want your chicken to be, and roll out into rough fillet shapes. Don't make them too perfect. Place them on a baking tray lined with baking paper.

Preheat the oven to 180°C (360°F) and bake for about 15 minutes, or until the surface of the chicken begins to turn a light golden brown.

While the fillets are cooking, combine all the poaching liquid ingredients in a large saucepan and bring to the boil.

Once the fillets are ready, turn the poaching liquid down to a very low simmer, add the chicken fillets and poach for 20 minutes.

Carefully remove, place back on the baking tray covered with a piece of baking paper and refrigerate for a minimum of 6 hours before using.

Meanwhile, make the sauce. In a large frying pan, melt the butter over a medium heat, then add the shallot and a pinch of salt. Cook until the shallot begins to soften, then add the garlic and cook for another minute before adding the flour.

Cook the flour over a low heat, stirring constantly, till you have a blond roux, about 2–3 minutes.

Slowly pour in the chicken stock, whisking constantly to avoid lumps.

Add the lemon juice and capers, and gently simmer until the sauce is thickened and glossy. Stir through the parsley and season well.

To serve, dust the fillets in seasoned flour, drizzle with a little oil and fry in a hot frying pan for a few minutes on each side until golden, then drop the fillets into the sauce. Turn to fully coat the fillets, then place on a plate and pour the remaining sauce over the top.

MEATBALLS

Balls

150 g (5½ oz) stale bread, crusts removed and torn

125 ml (4 fl oz/½ cup) soy milk

400 g (14 oz) fresh vegan mince

1 brown onion, grated and squeezed of extra moisture

2 garlic cloves, finely grated

1 tablespoon cornflour (cornstarch)

1 teaspoon fennel seeds, crushed

½ teaspoon dried oregano

½ teaspoon chilli flakes, or more to taste

Sauce

60 ml (2 fl oz/¼ cup) extra-virgin olive oil, plus 1 tablespoon extra

1 brown onion, finely diced

1 celery stalk, finely diced

1 small carrot, finely diced

3 garlic cloves, minced

2 tablespoons tomato paste (concentrated puree)

250 ml (8½ fl oz/1 cup) white wine

250 ml (8½ fl oz/1 cup) vegan beef or vegetable stock

420 g (15 oz) Passata (page 16)

1 bay leaf

2 thyme sprigs

1 red chilli, split lengthways, or chilli flakes, to taste

¼ bunch of roughly chopped parsley

It was a toss-up whether we put this in mains or the Building Blocks section. Meatballs can be used in so many ways. Throw them in spaghetti for dinner, or put them in a roll for lunch the next day. The world is your meatball.

To make the meatballs, put the bread in a large bowl and pour the soy milk on top. Squish together with your hands, then leave to soften for about 10 minutes.

Once the bread is fully softened, add the remaining meatball ingredients and mix very well to combine.

Roll into whatever size meatballs you like, placing them on a plate or tray as you go.

To make the sauce, heat the oil in a shallow dutch oven over a medium heat and, once hot, drop in the onion, celery and carrot along with a pinch of salt and cook until they begin to soften, about 5 minutes.

Add the garlic and cook for another minute, then stir in the tomato paste and cook for another minute.

Deglaze with the wine and simmer until reduced by half, then pour in the stock and passata. Add the bay leaf, thyme and chilli. Season well, then stir to combine. Simmer over a low heat while you cook off the meatballs.

Heat the extra 1 tablespoon oil in a large frying pan set over a medium–high heat and brown the meatballs on all sides. (Work in batches so you don't overcrowd the pan.) You're not looking to fully cook the meatballs at this point, just seal them off.

Once all the meatballs are browned, drop them into the sauce. Stir gently to coat, then cover the pan with a lid. Reduce the heat to low and simmer for 15–20 minutes, stirring occasionally.

To finish, stir through the parsley and check the seasoning. Serve on polenta, through spaghetti or in a sandwich.

CHICKPEAS & RAPA

1 large bunch of rapa, tough ends trimmed, washed well

60 ml (2 fl oz/¼ cup) extra-virgin olive oil, plus extra for drizzling

4 garlic cloves, thinly sliced

½ teaspoon chilli flakes

500 g (1 lb 2 oz) chickpeas, either freshly cooked or tinned and drained

1 tablespoon vegan fish sauce (optional)

juice of ½ lemon

Vibrant, green vegetables are overrated. If you make this recipe and your greens aren't grey, soggy and completely devoid of structure, you haven't cooked them long enough. Soggy greens for lyfe!

Bring a large saucepan of salted water to the boil. Add the rapa and blanch for 5 minutes, then drain in a colander, reserving 250 ml (8½ fl oz/1 cup) of the cooking liquid. Squeeze out the excess water, then cut into large pieces about 10 cm (4 in) long.

Heat the olive oil in a large frying pan over a medium heat. Add the garlic and chilli flakes and cook until lightly golden, then add the chickpeas and stir to coat in the oil. Carefully drop in the rapa – it will spit at you a little if it's too wet. Toss the pan to evenly combine all the ingredients and loosen up the rapa.

Pour in the reserved cooking water, fish sauce and lemon juice. Cook over a medium heat for 5 minutes, stirring often until most of the liquid has been absorbed.

Serve topped with extra olive oil.

CANEDERLI

320 g (11½ oz) stale bread, torn into small pieces

200 ml (7 fl oz) tepid soy milk

2 tablespoons extra-virgin olive oil

120 g (4½ oz) brown onion, finely diced

10 g (¼ oz) dried porcini mushrooms, rehydrated in boiling water for 30 minutes

80 ml (2½ fl oz/⅓ cup) aquafaba

40 g (1½ oz) cornflour (cornstarch)

½ teaspoon black salt

½ teaspoon smoked paprika

Brodo (page 104), to serve (optional)

This dumpling is a sponge for flavour. Serve it with the Brodo (page 104) for maximum enjoyment.

Place the bread in a large bowl and pour the soy milk over the top. Mix using your hands until well combined. Set aside to hydrate while you cook the onion.

Heat the olive oil in a small frying pan over a medium heat and fry the onion with a pinch of salt until soft and lightly golden brown. Add the rehydrated porcini and cook for a further minute.

Transfer the cooked onion and mushrooms to the bread mixture, along with the remaining ingredients and mix with your hands until well-combined. Season to taste.

Bring a large saucepan of salted water to the boil. While the water is boiling, roll the mixture into four large balls.

Once the water has come to the boil, reduce the heat to medium and drop the dumplings in. Don't overcrowd the pot, so cook in batches of two if needed.

Simmer for about 15 minutes, or until they float. Carefully remove the dumplings from the saucepan and serve in brodo.

BRAISED MUSHROOMS & RADICCHIO

60 ml (2 fl oz/¼ cup) extra-virgin olive oil, plus extra for drizzling

1 brown onion, finely diced

300 g (10½ oz) button mushrooms, thickly sliced

½ small fennel bulb, core removed and thinly sliced

4 garlic cloves, minced

½ head radicchio, core removed and cut into large chunks

1 rosemary sprig

1 bay leaf

125 ml (4 fl oz/½ cup) white wine

400 g (14 oz) cooked cannellini beans, fresh or tinned and drained

500 ml (17 fl oz/2 cups) vegan chicken or vegetable stock

2 tablespoons vegan butter

50 g (1¾ oz/½ cup) grated vegan parmesan, plus extra to serve

handful of chopped parsley, to garnish

This is peak winter. Big comfort. Get it in ya'. It's also great stirred through pasta or over soft polenta.

Heat the olive oil in a large pan over a medium heat. Add the diced onion with a big pinch of salt and cook for a few minutes, or until beginning to soften.

Throw in the sliced mushrooms and cook until they start to turn golden.

Add the fennel to the pan and cook for a few minutes before adding the garlic, then cook for another minute. Season with salt and pepper.

Scatter the chopped radicchio into the pan and stir well to separate and coat, then add the rosemary and bay leaf.

Pour in the white wine and simmer until reduced by half, then add the drained beans. Stir to combine, then add the stock and simmer over a medium–low heat until the liquid has reduced by half.

To finish the sauce, add the butter and parmesan and stir until melted and combined. Sprinkle the parsley over the top and stir through.

Serve with extra parmesan and a splash of olive oil.

RISOTTO MILANESE

This has a bit more going on than a regular risotto milanese. This is the version I serve at Alibi in Sydney pumped up with pureed and pickled pumpkin, and people go nuts for it. Come to think of it, is it even Milanese anymore?

Risotto milanese

2 litres (68 fl oz/8 cups) vegan chicken or vegetable stock

100 g (3½ oz) vegan butter

30 ml (1 fl oz) extra-virgin olive oil

1 small brown onion, finely diced

300 g (10½ oz) arborio rice

125 ml (4 fl oz/½ cup) dry white wine

½ teaspoon saffron threads

50 g (1¾ oz/½ cup) grated vegan parmesan

Pumpkin variation

250 g (9 oz) pumpkin, peeled

2 shallots

1 garlic clove, peeled

vegetable stock, to cover

60 ml (2 fl oz/¼ cup) vegan cream or soy milk

Bring the stock to the boil in a large saucepan, then turn the heat down very low and cover with a lid to keep warm.

Heat 50 g (1¾ oz) of butter and the oil in a large, heavy-based frying pan over a medium heat, then add the onion with a pinch of salt. Cook until the onion is soft and translucent – avoid any colour.

Next, add the rice and cook for about 2 minutes, stirring constantly until the outside of the grains become translucent and you can only see a small speck of opaque white in the centre.

Increase the heat to medium–high and pour in the wine, stir, and allow to completely evaporate.

Add the warm stock, two ladles at a time. Lower the heat to medium and stir fairly consistently until the stock has been almost fully absorbed (don't let it dry out though as this can lead to the rice breaking). Continue adding the stock and stirring until the rice is cooked. You may not need all the stock, but it's best to have it ready in case you do.

When you add your final ladle of stock, crumble in the saffron threads. Continue stirring gently for the final few minutes. The entire cooking process should take about 15 minutes.

Once the risotto is cooked, take the pan off the heat and drop in the remaining 50 g (1¾ oz) butter and the grated parmesan. Stir through and cover the pan with a lid or a tea (dish) towel.

You want silky, slightly runny risotto. If you can pick up a clump with a fork, add more stock.

Pumpkin variation

Place the pumpkin, shallots, garlic and enough vegetable stock to cover in a small saucepan and bring to a boil. Simmer until the pumpkin is soft, about 7 minutes. Remove from the heat and add in your cream or soy milk. Blend until smooth with a stick blender and season to taste.

My Spanish grandparents lived in Preston and my Aussie nan had a boutique in the market, so I spent a lot of time going to WOG (Welcomed Overseas Guest) bakeries in the area, thinking the cakes and pastries I was eating were Spanish. They were not! It wasn't until I was twelve or so that I realised all these desserts were Italian. Of course they were! Crostoli, peach cookies, sfogliatelle – they're all Italian.

When I was a kid and went to birthday parties for anyone of European descent, you bet there was one of those almond-covered, strawberry and chocolate-topped monstrosities standing in for birthday cake. I despised them! Back then, most of the continental-style cakes were packed full of booze, and I reckon they fed it to us kids so we'd all pass out instead of bounce off the walls from a sugar rush. Well done, Mum!

So, while these sweets are not from my heritage, they're a huge part of my food memories. They're as much a part of my blood as they are Italians', which is probably why this chapter is so unapologetically long. I genuinely adore each and every one of the desserts in this chapter, so I had to include them all. I hope you love them as much as I do.

DOLCI

ANGINETTI COOKIES

100 g (3½ oz) vegan butter
140 g (5 oz) caster (superfine) sugar
10 g (¼ oz) egg replacer
35 g (1¼ oz) cold water
1½ teaspoons vanilla extract
½–1 teaspoon anise extract
50 g (1¾ oz) extra-virgin olive oil
40 g (1½ oz) soy milk
300 g (10½ oz/2 cups) plain
(all-purpose) flour
½ teaspoon baking powder
pinch of salt

Lemon glaze

200 g (7 oz) icing (confectioners')
sugar
70 g (2½ oz) lemon juice

These cookies are the strongest memory from my childhood. I don't know where my mum used to get them, they'd just show up. The combination of anise and lemon is just perfect.

Cream the butter and sugar in a bowl with either a wooden spoon or an electric mixer until light and fluffy.

In a small bowl, combine the egg replacer with the cold water and stir well to combine.

Add the vanilla, anise, olive oil and soy milk and beat for another minute to incorporate.

Sift the flour and baking powder over the creamed butter mixture, then add the salt. Mix to combine.

The dough should be fairly soft, but not sticky. If it is, add a little more flour, 1 tablespoon at a time.

Wrap the dough in plastic wrap and refrigerate for at least 1 hour, or you can even make this the day before.

When ready to bake, preheat the oven to 160°C (320°F).

To make the cookies, cut the dough into twelve or so evenly sized pieces, then evenly roll into 15 cm (6 in) ropes. Twist to form your desired shape and place on a baking tray lined with baking paper.

Bake for 10–12 minutes or until the bottoms of the cookies are very lightly golden.

Remove from the oven and allow to cool on the tray before removing.

Once the cookies have cooled, make the lemon glaze by sifting the icing sugar into a bowl and stirring through enough lemon juice to make an opaque and runny mixture.

Grab the cookies and dip the entire top of each cookie into the glaze, then place on a cooling rack, bottom side down, and allow any excess glaze to drip off. Store in an airtight container for up to 1 week.

BOMBOLONI

10 g (¼ oz) yeast

100 g (3½ oz) tepid water

100 g (3½ oz) caster (superfine) sugar

5 teaspoons egg replacer

150 g (5½ oz) cold water

1 kg (2 lb 3 oz) plain (all-purpose) flour, plus extra for dusting

10 g (¼ oz) salt

300 g (10½ oz) soy milk

80 g (2¾ oz) cold vegan butter, cut into thin pieces

zest of 1 lemon

vegetable oil, for deep-frying

icing (confectioners') sugar, to coat

Not-Nutella (page 68), to fill (optional)

When people think about doughnuts, they automatically think about the American variety. When I think about doughnuts, my mind goes straight to these bomboloni. They can be filled with anything: classically, jam or custard. Feel free to stuff them with whatever you like within reason. Maybe not bolognese sauce. Let me know how it goes if you do.

Place the yeast, water and a teaspoon of the sugar in a small bowl and stir well to combine. Allow to sit for 5 minutes, or until the mixture is bubbly.

In another small bowl, whisk together the egg replacer and cold water, then set aside.

Place the flour, salt and the rest of the sugar in the bowl of a stand mixer fitted with the dough hook attachment. Mix on low speed for 10 seconds to combine.

Pour the yeast mixture, soy milk and egg replacer mixture into the stand mixer and mix on low speed until the liquid is completely incorporated. If the mixture seems too sticky, add a little extra flour, 1 tablespoon at a time, until the dough begins to pull away from the side of the bowl and becomes smooth. This will take about 5–7 minutes.

Add half of the butter and the lemon zest to the dough, increase the speed to medium and mix until it's fully incorporated before adding the remaining butter.

At this stage the dough may look like it doesn't want to take in the butter, but give it some time. If necessary, add a little extra flour, 1 tablespoon at a time, until the dough just begins to pull away from the side of the bowl again.

Knead for a final 4 minutes on medium speed, or until the dough is very soft, smooth and elastic. Place in a bowl that has been sprayed or wiped with oil and cover with a tea (dish) towel or plastic wrap. Set aside to prove in a warm place until doubled in size. This could take anywhere between 1–2 hours depending on the temperature of the room.

Once proved, knock back the dough by punching it right in the middle.

At this point you can continue making the bomboloni, or place the knocked-back dough in the fridge to cold-ferment overnight. This will give the doughnuts a much more developed flavour and texture. If you choose to cold-ferment, remove the dough from the fridge and bring to room temperature before continuing with the recipe (this will take about 1 hour).

Dust your work surface with flour then dump the dough on top and cut into twelve even pieces. Bomboloni are traditionally quite large doughnuts, but feel free to make them smaller if that's what you'd prefer.

To shape, pinch the corners together to create a ball, then gently roll the dough on a smooth surface to blend out the seams until you get a smooth, round dough ball. Place the ball onto a tray lined with baking paper and sprayed with oil. Repeat with the remaining dough.

Cover loosely with plastic wrap and leave to prove again until the doughnuts have almost doubled in size. This will take anywhere between 40 minutes and 1½ hours. When ready, the dough should feel very soft and bounce back slowly when pressed with your finger.

Heat enough oil for deep-frying in a large, heavy-based saucepan or deep-fryer. It should come about 10 cm (4 in) up the side of the pot. Heat to 170°C (340°F).

Carefully drop a few doughnuts at a time into the oil, making sure not to overcrowd the pan. They need to have enough room to float freely and expand. Fry the doughnuts for approximately 3–5 minutes, flipping every 15 seconds for the first minute to ensure they evenly brown, before frying for a further 1½ minutes on each side. Obviously, if you decide to make smaller doughnuts the cooking time will be slightly shorter, so just go on the colour and make sure you have a beautiful golden brown on both sides.

Test one by breaking it in half to make sure they are cooked through. Transfer to paper towel and allow to cool slightly.

Dust the doughnuts in icing sugar to coat.

Fill with jam, custard or Not-Nutella.

CARTELLATE

250 g (9 oz/1⅔ cups) plain
    (all-purpose) flour
¼ teaspoon salt
150 ml (5 fl oz) white wine
50 ml (1¾ fl oz) extra-virgin olive oil
vegetable oil, for deep-frying
250 ml (8½ fl oz/1 cup) vincotto
icing (confectioners') sugar, to serve
ground cinnamon, to serve

I haven't given you a recipe for cannoli, but, hot tip: this dough can be used to make it. There is a bit of faffing about with these. If you have a pasta machine, it will make your life easier, but it is certainly not a requirement. Vincotto used to be hard to find, but these days you can get it in most major supermarkets. It's basically the leftover grape skins from winemaking that have been boiled down into a syrup. These are perfect with coffee.

Add the flour and salt to a bowl and mix with your hands to combine. Create a well in the middle and pour in the wine and oil. Mix until everything comes together, then turn out onto a bench and knead for about 3 minutes, or until you have a smooth but slightly firm dough.

Wrap in plastic wrap and rest for at least 30 minutes. (This can be done the day before and stored in the fridge. Just bring to room temperature and re-knead for 1 minute to bring together before rolling if doing this.)

Once the dough has rested, cut into four pieces and roll out until the dough is about 2 mm (1/16 in) thick. This is best done with a pasta roller, but you can do it with a rolling pin. Once the dough is rolled, cut it into strips about 60 cm (23½ in) long and 3 cm (1¼ in) wide with the notched dough-cutting wheel.

Fold the strips in half so the two notched edges meet, lightly press down and form rough rosettes. Starting from the end, roll the strips on themselves by pinching the edges. Place on a tray and let them sit, uncovered, to dry for at least 2 hours, or even overnight.

When you're ready to fry them, heat enough oil for deep-frying in a large saucepan or deep-fryer until it reaches 160°C (320°F) and fry for around 2 minutes, turning once, or until they turn a golden brown. Drain on paper towel and cool completely.

In a small saucepan, simmer the vincotto over a medium heat until reduced by half. It should be thick and syrupy. Dip the cartelatte in the vincotto until fully covered.

To finish, dust with icing sugar and a sprinkle of cinnamon.

Note
If forming the dough into rosettes is too tricky, you can just fry these in strips and they're just as good.

CHOCOLATE HAZELNUT WAFERS

1 × 150 g (5½ oz) packet wafer sheets (you won't need to use the whole packet, just 2 sheets)

Filling

1 litre (34 fl oz/4 cups) soy milk

200 g (7 oz) icing mixture (not icing/confectioners' sugar)

150 g (5½ oz) vegan dark chocolate chips

50 g (1¾ oz) ground hazelnuts, toasted

salt flakes, to taste

The Aussie kids had Tiny Teddies in their lunchboxes, I had wafers, and I was happy about it. I make this recipe infinitely easier with pre-made wafer sheets. Do not try to make your own at home. I wouldn't either. It's not worth the sweat and tears.

Add the soy milk and icing mixture to a heavy-based saucepan over a low heat and whisk to combine.

You need to make sure that the heat is as low as possible and keep an eye on the pan so that it doesn't boil over. To properly reduce the milk to the correct consistency it needs long and slow cooking, stirring every 5 minutes or so.

Simmer until the milk has reduced to approximately 200 ml (7 fl oz) and is a dark caramel colour. This can take over an hour, so stick with it.

Once you have the perfect caramel, take the pan off the heat and add your choc chips, ground hazelnuts and salt. Stir until the chocolate is fully melted.

To build, use an offset spatula and thinly spread the chocolate mixture over the first sheet of wafer. Use enough to fill all the holes in the wafer and to thinly coat the entire surface. Place another wafer sheet on top.

Repeat the layers until all the chocolate has been used. Press down gently on each wafer sheet to stick the layers together.

Using a serrated knife, cut into whatever size you prefer, either large fingers or small squares. Store in an airtight container. These are best eaten on the day they're made.

Use the rest of the wafer sheets in your ice cream sundaes or to make more wafers.

CHOCOLATE TORTA

400 g (14 oz) vegan dark chocolate chips, or dark chocolate bar cut into small pieces

160 g (5½ oz) soy milk

2½ teaspoons baking powder

½ teaspoon bicarbonate of soda (baking soda)

1 tablespoon apple-cider vinegar

1 tablespoon vanilla extract or paste

250 g (9 oz) fine almond meal

140 g (5 oz) brown sugar

25 g (1 oz) dark cocoa powder, plus extra for dusting

½ teaspoon ground cinnamon

50 g (1¾ oz) cornflour (cornstarch)

1 teaspoon salt flakes

2 teaspoons instant coffee powder

This is really simple to make, but no one would ever know. It's super indulgent, especially served warm. If you want to show people you know what you're doing in the kitchen, serve drizzled with olive oil and a bit of Salt Bae.

Preheat the oven to 160°C (320°F). Grease and line a 20 cm (8 in) round springform cake tin.

Add the chocolate to a heatproof bowl and place over a saucepan filled about halfway with water – make sure the water doesn't touch the bowl. Place over a low heat and stir the chocolate with a spatula until fully melted. Remove from the heat and set aside.

While the chocolate is cooling, combine the soy milk, baking powder, bicarb' and vinegar in a jug and whisk well. Set aside to allow the vinegar to activate the raising agents for about 2 minutes.

Add all the ingredients to the slightly cooled chocolate mixture and fold through to combine. Don't overmix.

Pour the cake batter into the prepared cake tin and bake for 35–40 minutes. The cake is ready when a skewer inserted in the middle of the cake comes out coated with a little wet batter. It will firm up quite a lot as it cools.

Allow the cake to come to room temperature before removing from the tin. Dust heavily with cocoa powder before cutting.

NOUGAT

450 g (1 lb) caster (superfine) sugar

80 ml (2½ fl oz/⅓ cup) water

500 g (1 lb 2 oz) brown rice syrup or glucose syrup

80 ml (2½ fl oz/⅓ cup) aquafaba

pinch of cream of tartar

1 teaspoon vanilla extract

150 g (5½ oz) whole almonds, roasted

50 g (1¾ oz) whole pistachio nuts, roasted

rice paper (optional)

melted vegan chocolate (optional)

Are you game enough to make this? Only the hardcore ones will. If you don't have a sugar thermometer, don't even bother. Trust me, I learned the hard way so you don't have to.

Grease and line a 20 × 30 cm (8 × 12 in) baking tin.

Heat the sugar, water and brown rice syrup in a saucepan over a medium heat. Stir occasionally and brush down the sides of the saucepan with a wet pastry brush until the sugar dissolves. It takes a while.

Place a sugar thermometer in the saucepan, increase the heat and bring to the boil, but don't stir.

Whisk the aquafaba to stiff peaks in a stand mixer or using an electric mixer, adding the cream of tartar halfway through.

When the syrup reaches 150°C (300°F), gently pour it into the whisked aquafaba in a thin steady stream with the motor still going on medium speed. Continue mixing until the mix looks thick and glossy.

Add the vanilla and beat until just combined.

Stir in the almonds and pistachio nuts by hand using a wooden spoon or spatula. Be careful, as the sides of the bowl will be very hot, but work quickly before the nougat sets.

If using the rice paper, cut two sheets to fit your tin. Place one sheet in the base of the tin. Pour the nougat over the rice paper and smooth it out using a clean spatula (it helps if the spatula has been dipped in hot water). Place the other sheet of rice paper on top and press down. Allow to set at room temperature until firm, about 2 hours. Once set, using a knife that has been dipped in hot water, cut into eight bars. This is also great as a little bite-sized snack if you want to cut it into smaller pieces.

If you like, dip one side of the bar in melted chocolate and allow to set on a cooling rack.

Store in an airtight container for up to 1 month.

MASCARPONE &
RICOTTA CHEESECAKE

70 g (2½ oz) melted vegan butter

150 g (5½ oz) shop-bought plain biscuits, crushed

15 g (½ oz) egg replacer

100 g (3½ oz) cold water

225 g (8 oz) vegan cream cheese

225 g (8 oz) Mascarpone (page 24)

200 g (7 oz) Ricotta (page 23)

150 g (5½ oz) caster (superfine) sugar

50 g (1¾ oz) brown sugar

zest and juice of 1 large lemon

2 tablespoons cornflour (cornstarch)

1 tablespoon vanilla paste or extract

½ teaspoon salt

This is what the recipes from the Building Blocks chapter were for. Use them wisely.

Preheat the oven to 170°C (340°F). Grease and line a 22 cm (8¾ in) round springform cake tin.

To make the biscuit base, pour the melted butter into a bowl containing the crushed biscuits and mix well to combine. Pour the biscuit base mixture into the cake tin, press down with the bottom of a cup and refrigerate while you make the cheesecake filling.

In another small bowl, combine the egg replacer and water, whisking well to combine, then put aside.

Beat the cream cheese until smooth in the bowl of a stand mixer fitted with the paddle attachment on medium speed.

Add the mascarpone and ricotta and mix again but on low speed.

Once all three cheeses are combined, add the remaining ingredients and beat on medium speed until smooth and combined.

Pour the filling into the tin on top of the biscuit base and bake for about 50 minutes to 1 hour. To test if it's ready, jiggle the tin – you want a slightly wobbly centre and the top should be lightly golden.

Once ready, turn off the oven and slightly crack open the door. Leave the cheesecake inside until cooled to room temperature.

Refrigerate for at least 4 hours, or until firm, before serving.

ORANGE POLENTA CAKE

Cake

2 small oranges (approx. 400 g/14 oz)

150 g (5½ oz) caster (superfine) sugar

170 g (6 oz) fine polenta

60 g (2 oz) almond meal

180 g (6½ oz) plain (all-purpose) flour

2 teaspoons baking powder

½ teaspoon bicarbonate of soda (baking soda)

½ teaspoon salt

½ teaspoon ground fennel seeds

220 ml (7½ fl oz) soy milk

1 teaspoon white-wine or apple-cider vinegar

50 ml (1¾ fl oz) extra-virgin olive oil

Syrup

60 g (2 oz) orange juice

40 g (1½ oz) lemon juice

60 g (2 oz) caster (superfine) sugar

I love whole orange cakes. There is something so cool about boiling whole oranges. Depending on the time of year, you can substitute your favourite citrus. I have done this with kumquats and it was incredible. Just ensure that your citrus weighs 400 g (14 oz).

Place the 2 whole oranges in a saucepan and cover with water. Bring to the boil over a high heat, then simmer gently for 45 minutes to 1 hour, or until very soft, then drain.

Cut the oranges into quarters, remove any seeds and then blend in a food processor with the sugar until it forms a paste. Set aside.

Preheat the oven to 180°C (360°F) and prepare a 22 cm (8¾ in) round springform cake tin. Line the base with baking paper and brush or spray the sides well with oil or melted butter.

In a large mixing bowl combine the polenta, almond meal, flour, baking powder, bicarb', salt and ground fennel seeds.

In a jug or small bowl, mix together the soy milk and vinegar and allow to thicken for 1 minute before adding the oil.

Create a well in the centre of the polenta mix and add the orange puree and thickened soy milk. Mix well, then pour the batter into the cake tin and even out the surface.

Bake for 45–50 minutes, or until a skewer inserted in the middle of the cake comes out fairly clean.

Halfway through baking (about 20 minutes in), add all the syrup ingredients to a small saucepan and bring to the boil, stirring to dissolve the sugar. Once dissolved, remove from the heat.

When the cake is baked, remove from the oven and poke a few holes in the surface with a skewer. Drizzle the syrup over the cake, then allow to cool slightly before removing from the tin.

PEACH COOKIES

200 ml (7 fl oz) Alkermes, peach schnapps or Campari sweetened with peach nectar

Cookies

125 g (4½ oz/½ cup) vegan butter, softened

100 g (3½ oz) caster (superfine) sugar

40 g (1½ oz) soy milk

1 teaspoon vanilla extract

½–1 teaspoon almond extract

150 g (5½ oz/1 cup) plain (all-purpose) flour

8 g (¼ oz/1½ teaspoons) baking powder

pinch of salt

Filling

255 g (9 oz) soy milk

50 g (1¾ oz) caster (superfine) sugar, plus extra for coating

½ teaspoon vanilla extract

zest of ½ lemon

50 g (1¾ oz) custard powder

When I was younger, I used to think these were the cutest cookies that ever existed and nothing has changed. You can use fresh mint leaves as garnish, but for authenticity, artificial greenery is recommended. Alkermes is the liqueur used in this recipe and can be found in specialty grocers. If you can't find it, use peach schnapps or Campari with a splash of peach nectar instead. If you don't want them to contain booze, just soak them in peach nectar.

Preheat the oven to 170°C (340°F).

Cream the butter and sugar in a bowl with a wooden spoon until light and fluffy. Add the soy milk, vanilla and almond extracts, then combine.

Sift the flour, baking powder and salt over the butter mixture and mix to combine. The dough should be a tiny bit sticky. If needed, add a little extra flour. Wrap in plastic wrap and refrigerate for a minimum of 1 hour to firm up.

While the dough is chilling, make the filling.

Pour 175 g (6 oz) soy milk into a small saucepan, then add the sugar, vanilla extract and lemon zest. Bring to the boil, then turn the heat down to low and simmer.

In a small bowl, combine the custard powder with the remaining 80 g (2¾ oz) soy milk and mix to make a smooth paste, then whisk this mixture into the hot milk. Continue to cook over a low heat until thickened.

Pour the mixture into a bowl and cover with plastic wrap so that it doesn't form a skin, then refrigerate till cold.

Roll the mixture into sixteen equal-sized balls, then place on a baking tray lined with baking paper.

Bake for 8–10 minutes, or until the bottoms of the cookies are lightly golden.

While still warm, scoop out a small whole in the bottom of each cookie to allow for the filling.

Place the cooled filling in a piping (pastry) bag then snip the corner and fill the holes in the cookies with the filling. Press two together slightly.

Dip the outside in Alkermes, or the liqueur of your choice, then roll in caster sugar. Place, flat side down, on a cooling rack to allow the liqueur to absorb. Garnish with a leaf.

SFOGLIATELLE

To give you an idea of how long these take to make, it took me the entire run time of the Coronation to build them – not including the pastry, because I made it the day before. There are enough vegan cookbooks in the world with basic cake recipes that I think you deserve more. This is for people who are fairly confident in the kitchen and like a bit of a challenge. You're not going to find a vegan version of these anywhere, so making them at home is the only time you'll be able to try them. They will impress. Tag me if you make these.

icing (confectioners') sugar, for dusting

Pastry

120 g (4½ oz) water, plus extra if needed

20 g (¾ oz) agave or icing (confectioners') sugar

250 g (9 oz/1⅔ cups) plain (all-purpose) flour

¼ teaspoon salt

75 g (2¾ oz) vegan butter, room temperature

75 g (2¾ oz) vegetable shortening, room temperature (or replace with more butter if preferred)

Filling

125 ml (4 fl oz/½ cup) soy milk

40 g (1½ oz) sugar

½ teaspoon vanilla extract or paste

pinch of salt

40 g (1½ oz) fine semolina (not instant)

20 g (¾ oz) candied citrus peel

20 g (¾ oz) plain vegan yoghurt

⅛ teaspoon ground cinnamon

125 g (4½ oz/½ cup) Ricotta (page 23)

To make the pastry, measure the water into a small jug or bowl and dissolve the agave or icing sugar in it.

Combine the flour and salt in a bowl, then add the sweetened water. Using your hands, mix to create a stiff dough. If it's a little dry, gradually add more water, 1 tablespoon at a time.

Turn the dough out onto a bench and knead for 5–8 minutes, or until smooth and elastic. Wrap in plastic wrap and rest in the fridge for at least 2 hours (but this can be done the day before).

After the dough has rested, cut it into three pieces. If you have a pasta roller, it'll make rolling a whole lot easier. If not, get prepared for a workout.

If using a roller, start on the widest setting and pass a piece of dough through, just like if you were making pasta. Fold it in half and pass through again. Repeat the process, stepping down a notch at a time on the roller until you get to the thinnest setting. The final pastry should be close to 1 mm (1⁄16 in) thick and a large rectangle shape. Put to one side while you roll the remaining pieces of dough.

If using a rolling pin like I did while writing this recipe, roll one piece at a time onto an unfloured surface as thin as you possibly can, then gently pick up the edges and stretch, while giving it a little jiggle, almost like you're making filo.

In a small bowl, mix together the butter and vegetable shortening until well combined.

To create the layered pastry, place the first piece of rolled-out dough on your bench, then brush a thin layer of the butter/shortening mixture over the entire surface of the pastry.

Starting from the end closest to you (which should be the shorter side of the rectangle (approx. 20 cm/8 in across), start rolling up the pastry sheet as tightly as possible until you have a thin sausage shape. Leave it by the top of your bench and lay down the second sheet. Brush with

DOLCI

more of the butter mixture then place your first rolled dough sausage at the bottom of your second sheet, nearest you, and roll up again. Repeat a third time until you have one large log.

Once rolled, wrap the dough in plastic wrap and refrigerate for at least 2 hours to allow the butter mix to firm up.

While the dough is chilling, make the filling. Add the milk, sugar, vanilla and salt to a saucepan and bring to the boil over a high heat. Reduce the heat to medium, then slowly stream in the semolina. Stir constantly with a wooden spoon until it becomes very thick.

Transfer to a bowl and allow to cool.

Once the semolina has cooled, fold through the remaining ingredients until well combined, then place some plastic wrap directly on the surface of the mixture and refrigerate until cold.

Preheat the oven to 180°C (360°F).

Remove the rolled pastry from the fridge and unwrap. Cut into 1 cm (½ in) thick slices.

Dip your fingers in any remaining butter mixture, or grab a little extra if you used it all on the pastry. Rub it over your fingers and press the middle of the disc to create a cone shape. You should be able to see faint lines where you have created layers. Keep pushing the middle and turning the pastry disc slowly until your cone is about 8 cm (3¼ in) long.

Using a small spoon, fill the hollowed space with the chilled semolina mixture and press the edges of the pastry together to seal. Repeat until all the pastry and filling has been used.

Place on a baking tray lined with baking paper as you go, leaving a little space between each one.

Bake for 20–30 minutes, or until golden and crispy.

Once cooked, remove from the oven and allow to cool slightly before dusting with icing sugar.

If you've made it to the end, you are a superior being.

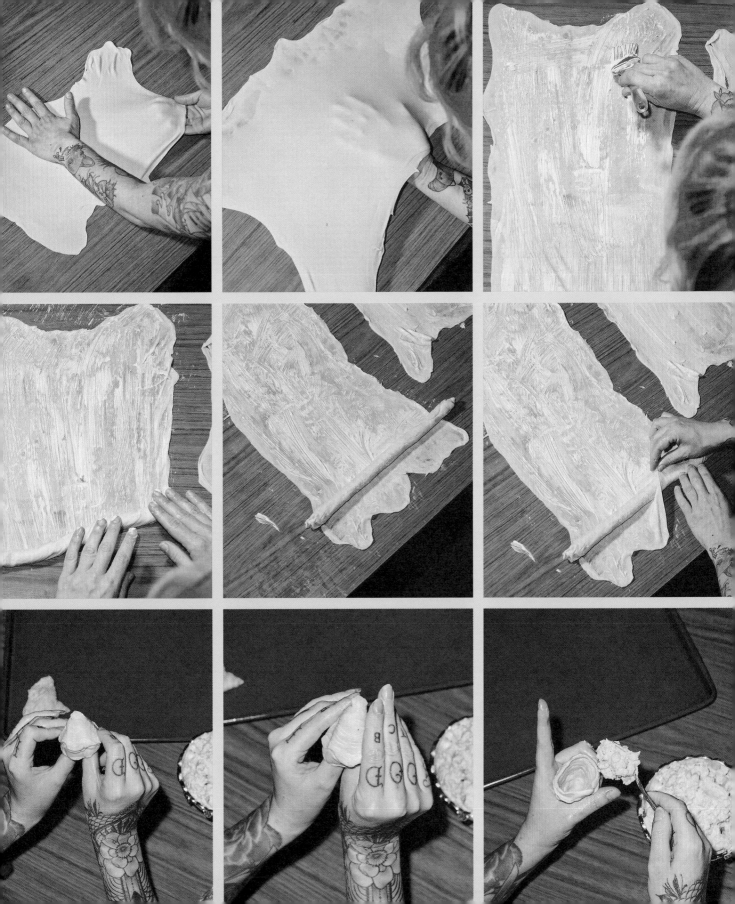

STRUFFOLI

In Italy, this is eaten during celebrations. I encourage you to decorate these with as many gaudy, tacky sprinkles as you can find. It's normally made with honey, but I've replaced this with an orange-scented syrup.

vegetable oil, for deep-frying

rainbow sprinkles, to garnish

Balls

80 g (2¾ oz) vegan butter

60 g (2 oz) silken tofu

10 g (¼ oz) egg replacer

140 g (5 oz) soy milk

400 g (14 oz) plain (all-purpose) flour, plus extra for dusting

¼ teaspoon salt

½ teaspoon bicarbonate of soda (baking soda)

pinch of ground turmeric

½ teaspoon ground anise (optional)

40 g (1½ oz) sugar

50 g (1¾ oz) anise liqueur

zest of ½ orange

Syrup

200 g (7 oz) caster (superfine) sugar

50 g (1¾ oz) orange juice

20 g (¾ oz) golden syrup

50 g (1¾ oz) water

Melt the butter in a microwave or in a small saucepan over low heat and allow to cool to room temperature.

Blend the silken tofu with the egg replacer and soy milk with a handheld or regular blender until smooth. Set aside.

Into a large mixing bowl, sift the flour, salt and bicarb', stir to combine, then add the turmeric and ground anise, if using.

Add the sugar and liqueur to the cooled melted butter, then pour into the flour mixture and stir to combine.

Make a well and pour in the tofu/egg mixture and orange zest. Mix with a spoon until it comes together, then turn out onto a floured bench and knead until a smooth dough forms.

Wrap in plastic wrap and rest for a minimum of 30 minutes.

While the dough is resting, make the syrup by combing all the ingredients in a saucepan and bringing to the boil over a medium heat. Once boiling, turn down the heat to low and simmer until all the sugar has melted. Remove from the heat.

Cut the dough into six pieces and roll into long ropes about 1 cm (½ in) thick. Cut into 1 cm (½ in) pieces then, using wet hands, roll into little balls.

Heat enough oil for deep-frying in a heavy-based saucepan until it reaches 160°C (320°F). Drop the dough balls into the oil in batches and fry for about 2 minutes, or until light golden brown. Remove from the oil with a slotted spoon and place in a large mixing bowl lined with paper towels. Repeat until all the balls have been fried.

Reheat the syrup over a medium heat until just warm and back to a honey-like consistency.

Remove the paper towel from underneath the fried dough balls and pour the warm syrup over the top.

Moving quickly, stack the dough balls onto a plate, forming a ring shape. This can be done by eye, or by placing a glass sprayed with non-stick cooking spray in the middle of a plate and forming the ring around the glass.

Finish by scattering over your favourite sprinkles.

TORTA DI RISO

200 g (7 oz) arborio rice (unwashed)

475 g (1 lb 1 oz) soy milk

1 bay leaf

40 g (1½ oz) egg replacer

400 g (14 oz) water

250 g (9 oz) caster (superfine) sugar

90 g (3 oz/¾ cup) custard powder

1 teaspoon ground cinnamon

100 g (3½ oz) rum

zest of 1 lemon

1 tablespoon vanilla extract

pinch of salt

400 g (14 oz) silken tofu, blended until smooth

Throughout my entire career, I have put rice pudding on the menu in the hope that some people might like it. I'm still trying. For the haters of rice pudding, this might be your gateway. Think rice pudding meets baked cheesecake. Now doesn't that sound better?

Preheat the oven to 180°C (360°F). Grease and line a 22 cm (8¾ in) springform cake tin with baking paper.

Bring a saucepan of lightly salted water to the boil and cook the rice for about 10 minutes, as you would pasta. Drain, then set aside. It should still be al dente.

Pour the soy milk into a small saucepan and add the bay leaf. Bring to the boil over a high heat, then remove from the heat and allow the bay leaf to infuse into the soy milk.

In a large mixing bowl, whisk together the egg replacer and water until fluffy, then add the sugar, custard powder, cinnamon, rum, zest, vanilla and a pinch of salt, and whisk again until well combined.

Remove the bay leaf from the soy milk. Add the warmed milk, blended tofu and the rice to the sugar mixture and stir by hand to combine. Pour into the tin and bake for 1 hour to 1¼ hours, or until golden brown with a few dark caramelised spots on top. It's ready when a skewer inserted in the middle comes out fairly clean.

Allow to cool completely before cutting. This can be served at room temperature or cold.

CASSATA

This is peak tacky European cake. When I was a kid, they were found in the freezers of European grocers in all sorts of lurid colours. A word of warning: this isn't the cake to make an hour before your guests arrive. This one is a project. A fun one. And it is well worth the effort. (This recipe is pictured on page 172.)

Cake

250 g (9 oz/1 cup) plain vegan yoghurt

160 g (5½ oz) caster (superfine) sugar

125 ml (4 fl oz/½ cup) vegetable oil

1 teaspoon baking powder

½ teaspoon bicarbonate of soda (baking soda)

pinch of salt

220 g (8 oz) plain (all-purpose) flour, plus extra for dusting

1½ teaspoons vanilla extract

Filling

300 g (10½ oz) vegan ricotta cheese, drained overnight in a piece of muslin (cheesecloth)

150 ml (5 fl oz) whipped vegan cream

75 g (2¾ oz) caster (superfine) sugar

¼ teaspoon almond extract

1 teaspoon vanilla paste or extract

90 g (3 oz/½ cup) vegan dark chocolate chips

20 g (¾ oz) chopped pistachio nuts

zest of ½ orange

Marzipan

300–400 g (10½–14 oz) marzipan

3–5 drops green food colouring (or colour of your choice)

Icing (confectioners') sugar, for dusting

Royal icing

25 g (1 oz) aquafaba

pinch of cream of tartar

175 g (6 oz) icing (confectioners') sugar

Decoration

mustard fruits

glacé cherries

candied citrus peel

Preheat the oven to 180°C (360°F).

Line 2 × 22 cm (8¾ in) springform cake tins with baking paper, then grease and dust with flour.

Start with the cake. Mix the yoghurt and sugar in a bowl until well combined. Add the oil, baking powder, bicarb' and salt to the yoghurt mixture and whisk well to combine, then leave to sit for 2 minutes, or until the yoghurt mixture becomes fluffy.

Sift the flour into the wet yoghurt mix and fold through. Mix in the vanilla and stir until you can no longer see any flour, but be careful not to overmix. A few lumps are okay.

Divide the cake batter evenly between the two tins and bake for 30–35 minutes, or until a skewer inserted in the middle of a cake comes out clean. Cool in the tin for 10 minutes before removing and cooling completely on a rack.

While the cake is cooling, make the filling. Place all the filling ingredients in a bowl and fold to combine, making sure to not deflate the cream. Store in the fridge until ready to assemble.

To build, find a circular mould that suits the size you would like to make your cassata, depending on whether you are making one large or multiple small cassatas. Use what you have at home – for this recipe, I used a large metal mixing bowl. Lightly spray the mould with oil and cover the surface with three layers of plastic wrap. This will make removing the cassata a hell of a lot easier.

For the first cake, which will be the top cake, place your mould, open side down, on the cake and trace a circle, 2½ cm (1 in) wider than the bowl. For your second cake, place the bowl on top of the cake again and this time, cut directly around the circumference of the mould. This will be the base of the cassata.

Place the top cake in the bowl, gently pressing it down to create a dome shape. Place your filling inside and roughly smooth out, then top with your base layer cake. Fold the plastic wrap that is hanging over the sides of the mould on top of the base layer and gently press down. Place in the freezer for 1 hour.

While the cassata is freezing, prepare the marzipan. Lightly dust a work surface with icing sugar. Knead the marzipan until it begins to soften, about 1 minute. Starting with three drops of green food colouring, knead until you achieve a uniform colour. Add more drops of food colouring if needed to achieve a bright green colour. Shape the marzipan into a ball.

Dust your work surface and a rolling pin with icing sugar. Roll out the marzipan into a 2 mm (⅛ in)-thick circle. If you are making smaller cassatas, you can also use a pasta roller to create a flat sheet and cut out small circles.

To make the royal icing, combine the aquafaba, cream of tartar and icing sugar. Pour into a piping (pastry) bag with a very fine round tip.

To finish, unmould the cassata, removing the plastic wrap, and carefully place onto a serving dish. If you are making smaller individual cassatas, this next step is easier if you place them onto a board and then transfer onto serving plates once decorated.

Gently pick up the rolled-out marzipan and place it over the cassata. Using your hands, smooth it out until there are no creases. Trim the excess from the base.

Decorating cassata can be whatever you want it to be. If you'd like to make it like I have here, begin by using the royal icing to create a large circle on top of the dome. Create petals coming a third of the way down the cassata. Pipe three dots between each petal and finish with the candied fruit.

Store in the fridge for up to 2 days. This can also be stored in the freezer and eaten frozen.

CONTINENTAL CAKE

The dreaded continental cake. Why adults forced this on children, I will never understand. As an adult, I love it, but that was after I developed a taste for alcohol. If there's a picture of cake in the dictionary of my mind, it's this one. Don't eat and drive.

Cake

375 g (13 oz/1½ cups) plain vegan yoghurt

240 g (8½ oz) caster (superfine) sugar

220 g (8 oz) vegan butter, melted and cooled

1 tablespoon vanilla extract

1–2 teaspoons almond extract

330 g (11½ oz) plain (all-purpose) flour

¼ teaspoon salt

1 teaspoon bicarbonate of soda (baking soda)

2 teaspoons baking powder

Italian pastry cream

1 litre (34 fl oz/4 cups) soy milk

¼ teaspoon salt

200 g (7 oz) caster (superfine) sugar

2 large strips of lemon zest

1 tablespoon vanilla paste or extract

200 g (7 oz) custard powder

80 g (2¾ oz) vegan dark chocolate chips

1–2 teaspoons strawberry extract

a few drops of red or pink food colouring

Rum syrup

125 ml (4 fl oz/½ cup) water

80–125 ml (2½–4 fl oz/⅓–½ cup) rum, depending on your preference

100 g (3½ oz) caster (superfine) sugar

Whipped cream icing

250 ml (8½ fl oz/1 cup) vegan whipping cream

40 g (1½ oz/⅓ cup) icing (confectioners') sugar

1 teaspoon vanilla extract

To decorate

maraschino cherries

90 g (3 oz/1 cup) flaked almonds, toasted

shaved vegan chocolate

Start by making the cake. Preheat the oven to 180°C (360°F). Grease and line two 22 cm (8¾ in) round springform cake tins with baking paper, then spray or brush with oil or butter.

In a bowl, whisk together the yoghurt and sugar until well combined.

Add the melted butter, vanilla and almond extracts and whisk.

Sift the flour, salt, bicarb' and baking powder into the bowl and fold through with a spatula. Don't overmix.

Divide the batter evenly between the two cake tins and bake for about 35 minutes, or until a skewer inserted in the middle of a cake comes out clean.

Remove from the oven and leave to cool in the tin for 15 minutes before removing and cooling on a rack.

Once cold, slice both cakes in half horizontally, so you have four even cake layers.

Next, make the pastry cream. In a large saucepan, whisk together 700 ml (23½ fl oz) of the soy milk with the salt, sugar, lemon zest and vanilla. Bring to the boil, then reduce the heat to low.

In a small bowl, whisk the remaining soy milk with the custard powder until a smooth paste forms, then whisk into the saucepan. Cook over a low heat until smooth and thick, then divide evenly between three bowls.

For the vanilla layer, leave the pastry cream as is. For the second, add the chocolate chips and stir through until melted. For the strawberry layer, add the strawberry extract and a few drops of colouring to achieve a pastel pink.

Cover each bowl with plastic wrap and refrigerate until cool. (This can be made the day before.)

Make a rum syrup by combining the water, rum and sugar in a small saucepan. Place over a low heat and stir to dissolve the sugar. Don't boil, as you want to keep the syrup boozy. Pour into a jug.

To make the whipped cream icing, put the cream, icing sugar and vanilla in a stand mixer fitted with the balloon attachment, or combine in a bowl and use an electric mixer, then beat to stiff peaks. Transfer to a bowl, cover and refrigerate until needed.

To assemble the cake, place a cake layer on a serving plate or cake wheel. Drizzle some of the rum syrup over the cake.

Use the vanilla pastry for the first layer and spread over the cake, leaving a 1 cm (½ in) border around the edge, then top with another cake layer, pressing down gently so it sticks to the pastry cream.

Drizzle more rum syrup over the second layer, then spread the strawberry pastry cream on top, again leaving a 1 cm (½ in) border.

Top with a third layer of cake, drizzle with the rum syrup, then cover with the chocolate pastry cream.

Top with the final layer of cake and drizzle with the remaining rum syrup. The cake should be fairly moist. Place in the fridge for 1 hour to firm up.

Fit a piping (pastry) bag with a star nozzle and fill it with one-quarter of the whipped cream. Set aside.

Use the remaining cream to cover the top and side of the cake. Use an offset spatula to get a smooth finish. Carefully press the flaked almonds onto the side of the cake.

Pipe rosettes on the top of the cake, around the entire edge, then place a cherry in the middle of each rosette.

Pile the shaved chocolate into the middle of the top of the cake and keep refrigerated until ready to serve.

Roll this out at christenings, communion, dinner with European in-laws, or to annoying children.

TIRAMISU

I'm not going to waste my time explaining what tiramisu is. All you need to know is – this recipe has crossed state lines. Vegans have travelled far and wide to eat my tiramisu. Now you can make it at home and take the credit for it. I don't mind. If you've managed to be prepared enough to make the Mascarpone on page 24, you'll be able to level up by switching half the cream for mascarpone.

cocoa powder, for dusting

Biscuit/cake layer

40 g (1½ oz) besan (chickpea flour)

300 ml (10 fl oz) hot water

340 g (12 oz) caster (superfine) sugar

60 ml (2 fl oz/¼ cup) vegetable oil

2 teaspoons vanilla extract

230 g (8 oz) plain (all-purpose) flour, or use gluten-free flour

18 g (¾ oz) baking powder

60 g (2 oz/½ cup) cornflour (cornstarch)

Custard

40 g (1½ oz/⅓ cup) custard powder

750 ml (25½ fl oz/3 cups) soy milk

100 g (3½ oz) caster (superfine) sugar

1 tablespoon vanilla extract

80 ml (2½ fl oz/⅓ cup) marsala

⅛ teaspoon black salt

Cream

750 ml (25½ fl oz/3 cups) vegan whipping cream (avoid coconut)

Coffee soak

300 ml (10 fl oz) black coffee

60 ml (2 fl oz/¼ cup) marsala, or your preferred liqueur

Start by making the biscuits or sheet cake. Preheat the oven to 170°C (340°F).

In a bowl, whisk together the chickpea flour and hot water. Add the sugar, oil and vanilla extract and whisk until light and fluffy.

Mix the flour, baking powder and cornflour in a small bowl, then gradually whisk into the wet mix until you have a smooth batter.

Pour into well-greased finger biscuit silicone moulds, or into a shallow baking tray lined with baking paper and bake for 10–12 minutes, or until lightly golden.

Leave to cool for 15 minutes before turning out onto a cooling rack. If you've baked the batter into one large sheet, cut into pieces to fit your serving dish.

To make the custard, mix the custard powder with a splash of the soy milk until you form a smooth paste. Whisk in the rest of the soy milk and the remaining ingredients until well combined.

Pour into a large saucepan and cook over a low heat until thick, whisking the whole time to avoid any lumps.

Pour into a bowl and place a piece of plastic wrap directly on the surface of the custard to prevent a skin forming. Allow to cool to room temperature. While the custard is cooling, whip the cream to medium-firm peaks.

Once cooled, give the custard a quick mix and gently fold through the whipped cream. Combine the coffee and marsala in a shallow bowl.

To build, soak your biscuits or cake pieces in the spiked coffee then cover the base of your dish with them.

Spoon over a thick layer of the custard on top, spreading it out evenly, then repeat the layers until you have used up all the ingredients. Finish with a layer of the custard, then dust liberally with cocoa powder and place in the fridge. Leave for a minimum of 4 hours before serving, overnight is best.

It's pretty damn hard to find some decent vegan gelato out there that doesn't just taste like soy or coconut milk. I used to think my gelato recipe was pretty awesome until I hired Josh Bosen as my head chef at Smith & Daughters. Sometimes, you just have to admit that someone is better than you at something and relinquish that section to them. So, while this is my book, the gelato recipes are Josh's. We use a Pacojet to make them in the restaurant, but Josh has developed these recipes to be churned in a domestic ice cream machine. Think of the gelato recipes as blank canvases that you can build and add to. We'll give you a few suggestions for variations, but you're only limited by your imagination.

If you have more of a spartan kitchen, stick to the granitas. I promise you they're just as satisfying.

GELATO & GRANITA

VANILLA GELATO BASE

350 g (12½ oz) oat milk

240 g (8½ oz) vegan cream

325 g (11½ oz) water

200 g (7 oz) caster (superfine) sugar

3–4 vanilla bean pods, cut in half, seeds scraped, or 1 tablespoon vanilla bean paste

Combine all the ingredients in a saucepan and whisk to combine. Set over a low heat and bring to a gentle simmer while stirring, then remove from the heat and leave to cool. Chill the mixture in the fridge.

Blend the chilled mixture with a handheld blender or high-speed blender until smooth, then pour into your ice cream machine of choice.

If you're using a benchtop mixer, set the machine to pre-chill then pour the mixture in and run the churning cycle until the gelato is frozen and mixed.

If you're using a stand mixer like Kenwood or KitchenAid with the gelato bowl attachment, freeze the bowl then add to the machine and mix on slow churn until frozen.

Store in the freezer for up to 3 months.

CHOCOLATE GELATO BASE

300 g (10½ oz) soy or oat milk

220 g (8 oz) vegan cream

80 g (2¾ oz/⅓ cup) caster (superfine) sugar

300 g (10½ oz) vegan dark chocolate chips (56% cocoa solids or higher)

Combine the milk, cream and sugar in a saucepan over a low heat.

Fill another saucepan about halfway with water and place a heatproof bowl on top. Add the chocolate and melt over a low heat, making sure the water doesn't touch the bottom of the bowl.

Bring the cream mixture to a gentle simmer, then pour it over the melted chocolate and mix to combine. Pour into a container and chill.

Blend the chilled mixture with a handheld blender or high-speed blender until smooth, then pour into your ice cream machine of choice.

If you're using a benchtop mixer, set the machine to pre-chill then pour the mixture in and run the churning cycle until the gelato is frozen and mixed.

If you're using a stand mixer like Kenwood or KitchenAid with the gelato bowl attachment, freeze the bowl then add to the machine and mix on slow churn until frozen.

Store in the freezer for up to 3 months.

BERRY GELATO

200 g (7 oz) soy milk
165 g (6 oz) vegan cream
100 g (3½ oz) caster (superfine) sugar
300 g (10½ oz) berries, pureed
50 g (1¾ oz) water

Combine all the ingredients in a saucepan and whisk to combine. Set over a low heat and bring to a gentle simmer while stirring.

Remove from the heat and let it cool, then pour the mixture into a container and chill.

Blend the chilled mixture with a handheld blender or high-speed blender until smooth, then pass through a fine-mesh sieve to remove any seeds. Pour into the ice cream machine of your choice.

If you're using a benchtop mixer, set the machine to pre-chill then pour the mixture in and run the churning cycle until the gelato is frozen and mixed.

If you're using a stand mixer like Kenwood or KitchenAid with the gelato bowl attachment, freeze the bowl then add to the machine and mix on slow churn until frozen.

Store in the freezer for up to 3 months.

MAKES 4–6

YOGHURT GELATO

200 g (7 oz) soy or oat milk
150 g (5½ oz) vegan cream
100 g (3½ oz) caster (superfine) sugar
50 g (1¾ oz) water
300 g (10½ oz) plain vegan yoghurt

Combine the milk, cream, sugar and water in a saucepan and whisk to combine. Set over a low heat and bring to a gentle simmer while stirring.

Remove from the heat and leave to cool. Once cool, mix in the yoghurt and chill the mixture.

Blend the chilled mixture with a handheld blender or high-speed blender until smooth, then pour into the ice cream machine of your choice.

If you're using a benchtop mixer, set the machine to pre-chill then pour the mixture in and run the churning cycle until the gelato is frozen and mixed.

If you're using a stand mixer like Kenwood or KitchenAid with the gelato bowl attachment, freeze the bowl then add to the machine and mix on slow churn until frozen.

Store in the freezer for up to 3 months.

BASIL GRANITA

250 g (9 oz) apple juice

250 g (9 oz) lemon juice, plus the zest

50 g (1¾ oz/1 cup) basil leaves
(approx. 30 leaves)

500 g (1 lb 2 oz) water

250 g (9 oz) caster (superfine) sugar

pinch of salt

Basil is used in a lot of savoury applications, but it is actually sweet, so it only makes sense to put it in a granita. I know what you're thinking. Don't think that.

Place the apple juice, lemon juice and zest, and the basil in a blender and blend for 15 seconds on high speed.

Pour the water, sugar and salt into a small saucepan and cook over a medium heat, stirring until the sugar has dissolved.

As soon as the sugar has dissolved, take off the heat and allow to cool for 30 minutes, then add to the blender and blend to incorporate.

Pour the liquid through a fine-mesh sieve into a shallow freezer-safe container.

Freeze for 2 hours, then remove and scrape with a fork. Place back in the freezer and freeze for a further 3 hours, scraping with a fork every 30 minutes to create a fluffy texture.

Store in the freezer until ready to serve. Fluff with a fork once more before eating. This can be stored in the freezer for up to 3 months.

CITRUS GRANITA

750 g (1 lb 11 oz) water

350 g (12½ oz) lemon juice, plus the zest from 2 lemons

250 g (9 oz) caster (superfine) sugar

Is there anything more satisfying than citrus granita on a hot day? I think not. Like the orange cake, feel free to substitute the citrus or combine them all. For me, lemon reigns supreme.

Add all the ingredients to a large saucepan and place over a medium heat, stirring until the sugar has dissolved.

As soon as the sugar has dissolved, remove from the heat and pour into a shallow freezer-safe container.

Freeze for 2 hours, then remove and scrape with a fork. Place back in the freezer and freeze for a further 3 hours, scraping with a fork every 30 minutes to create a fluffy texture.

Store in the freezer until ready to serve. Fluff with a fork one more time before eating. This can be stored in the freezer for up to 3 months.

PRICKLY PEAR GRANITA

20 prickly pears (to produce 650 g/
1 lb 7 oz juice; see method)
40 g (1½ oz) orange juice
60 g (2 oz) lemon juice
115 g (4 oz/½ cup) caster (superfine)
sugar

The colour alone is an excuse to make this.

Begin by juicing the prickly pears. Run them through a juicer if you have one, otherwise blend until smooth then pass through a fine-mesh sieve to remove the pulp.

Pour the prickly pear, orange and lemon juices into a saucepan with the sugar and cook over a medium heat, stirring until the sugar has dissolved.

As soon as the sugar has dissolved, take off the heat and pour the liquid into a shallow freezer-safe container.

Freeze for 2 hours, then remove and scrape with a fork. Place back in the freezer and freeze for a further 3 hours, scraping with a fork every 30 minutes to create a fluffy texture.

Store in the freezer until ready to serve. Fluff with a fork once more before eating. This can be stored in the freezer for up to 3 months.

TARTUFO

800 g (1 lb 12 oz) Chocolate gelato (page 208), or use pre-bought vegan chocolate gelato

4 maraschino cherries

300 g (10½ oz) vegan dark chocolate

100 g (3½ oz) refined coconut oil

50 g (1¾ oz) toasted hazelnuts, finely chopped

pinch of salt

This is another childhood classic. When we used to go to the local Italian restaurant, it was my ultimate dessert. I thought it was *so* fancy. Looking at it now, there is nothing fancy about it. There is just something about cracking through a hard, chocolate shell to reach the cherry in the middle. (I still never eat the cherry, but it wouldn't be tartufo without it.)

Roll the gelato into four large balls. Push a cherry into the centre of each ball, then smooth over to cover the hole. Place on a plate or tray and freeze for a minimum of 2 hours to firm up.

Once the gelato balls are very firm, place the chocolate and coconut oil in a heatproof bowl set over a saucepan of simmering water. Stir until melted and smooth, then stir through the hazelnuts and salt. Pour into a jug and set aside.

Place the gelato balls on a cooling rack, then pour the chocolate over to fully coat. Allow to set for a few minutes before removing from the rack and returning to the freezer until ready to serve.

ABOUT THE AUTHOR

A tour de force in vegetarian and vegan cooking, Shannon Martinez has been a chef in Melbourne kitchens for over 25 years. She is best known as the owner of Australia's most prolific plant-based business, Smith & Daughters, which resulted in the best-selling books *Smith & Daughters: A Cookbook (That Happens to be Vegan)*, *Smith & DELIcious: Food From Our Deli (That Happens to be Vegan)*, and *Vegan With Bite*. While Shannon eats meat, she has perfected her vegan repertoire and says this is what makes her food taste so good; she aims to replicate the flavours and textures of meat, rather than serving bland, predictable, vegan fare.

ACKNOWLEDGEMENTS

It's crazy to think that between the release of *Vegan With Bite* and *Vegan Italian Food* I've experienced cancer not once, but twice. So I guess it's safe to say that I have a lot more people to thank this time 'round.

To the medical team at Peter MacCallum Cancer Centre, thanks for keeping me alive – on multiple occasions. I guess when it really comes down to it, if it wasn't for you guys both this book and I might not be here today. So, thanks for that!

As always, the support of family, friends, staff and loyal customers is wholeheartedly appreciated. To my Hardie Grant team, thank you for your patience while I navigated cancer, surgeries, a pandemic and keeping multiple businesses open whilst trying to complete this book. If it wasn't for the help of my absolute dream team Ana, Simon, Vaughan, Bridget, KP and Ash, there is no way this book would be in your hands today.

I need to give a special shout out to some key players in my road to today. My mum, Richard, Antoni, Dayna, Jayden, Ness, Tamara, Deb, Emma, Jess, Jerry, Eliza, El, Josh, Phil, Rachel, Sean, Raz & Co, Curley and of course, my soul mate Sirus.

And to my beautiful nan, Noelie. This book is dedicated to you. I wish you could have seen it completed. I just know this one would have been your favourite. X

Let's hope the road to the next book is a little smoother.

Lots of love,

Shannon

INDEX

Published in 2024 by Hardie Grant Books,
an imprint of Hardie Grant Publishing

Hardie Grant Books (Melbourne)
Wurundjeri Country
Building 1, 658 Church Street
Richmond, Victoria 3121

Hardie Grant Books (North America)
2912 Telegraph Ave
Berkeley, California 94705

hardiegrant.com/books

Hardie Grant acknowledges the Traditional Owners of the Country on which we work, the Wurundjeri People of the Kulin Nation and the Gadigal People of the Eora Nation, and recognises their continuing connection to the land, waters and culture. We pay our respects to their Elders past and present.

A catalogue record for this book is available from the National Library of Australia

Vegan Italian Food
ISBN 978 1 74379 651 1
ISBN 978 1 76144 174 5 (ebook)

10 9 8 7 6 5 4 3 2 1

Publisher: Simon Davis
Head of Editorial: Jasmin Chua
Project Editor: Ana Jacobsen
Editor: Andrea O'Connor
Design Manager: Kristin Thomas
Designer: Vaughan Mossop
Typesetter: Hannah Schubert
Photographer: Kristoffer Paulsen
Stylist: Bridget Wald
Home Economist: Joshua Bosen
Head of Production: Todd Rechner
Production Controller: Jessica Harvie

Colour reproduction by Splitting Image Colour Studio
Printed in China by Leo Paper Products LTD.

MIX
Paper | Supporting responsible forestry
FSC® C020056

The paper this book is printed on is from FSC®-certified forests and other sources. FSC® promotes environmentally responsible, socially beneficial and economically viable management of the world's forests.